John Macready
Aviation Pioneer

At the Earth's Ceiling

*A celebration of the first
non-stop transcontinental flight
and the pioneer who made it happen.*

John Macready
Aviation Pioneer

At the Earth's Ceiling

*To Mary Ellen and Don — a bit
a aviation history for you!*

Sally Macready Wallace

by

Sally Macready Wallace

Sunflower University Press®

1531 Yuma • P. O. Box 1009 • Manhattan, Kansas 66505-1009 USA

Cover, by Mike Boss, Hill City, Kansas.

Technical Editor, Sonie Liebler

Layout, Lori L. Daniel

ISBN 0-89745-225-9

Sunflower University Press is a wholly-owned subsidiary
of the non-profit 501(c)3 Journal of the West, Inc.

To my husband Tom
For his patience, encouragement, ingenuity
and cooperative assistance, generously given
and for just being a wonderful guy

and to

Donald G. Foster
whose persistent and unflagging help gave
me the motivation to finish this book

The day may soon come when a flight from New York to San Francisco will be so familiar as to pass virtually unnoticed.

— *The New York Times*, May 4, 1923

Contents

Introduction   xiii

Chapter 1   Coast-to-Coast, Hour Zero   1
             The First Attempt to Leave Roosevelt Field, New York
             Beginnings — The Early Years in Searchlight, Nevada

Chapter 2   Coast-to-Coast, Hour One   16
             Takeoff from Roosevelt Field
             Up, Up, and Away — Flight Training at Rockwell,
                Gerstner, and Brooks Fields

Chapter 3   Coast-to-Coast, Hour Two   28
             Signs of Trouble
             Flying Blind — Pioneering Experiments and
                Developments at McCook Field

Chapter 4   Coast-to-Coast, Hour Seven   46
             Spotted Over Dayton
             Initial Attempts at Non-Stop Transcontinental Flight

Chapter 5   Coast-to-Coast, Hours Twelve to Fifteen   66
             In the Thick of the Night
             The Other Side of Heroism — Life as an
                Experimental Pilot

Chapter 6   Coast-to-Coast, Hour Seventeen   76
             As the Earth Rose into the Sky
             Joe Stiff — Parachuting in the Dark

Photo Scrapbook   80

Chapter 7   Coast-to-Coast, Hours Twenty, Twenty-Six   111
             — And Destination

Chapter 8   Down to Earth — Post-Flight   115

Chapter 9   A Bird's-Eye View — Photographing America   122
             from the Air

Chapter 10   One More River to Cross — The TransPacific Flight   142

Chapter 11   The End of an Era — The Final Years   153
             at McCook Field

Epilogue   162

Index   167

JOHN A. MACREADY
(1887-1979)

AVIATION ACHIEVEMENTS

1921 HIGH ALTITUDE RECORD 34,509 FEET
Over Dayton, Ohio, Orville Wright, Observer

1921 FIRST CROP DUSTING
August 31, 1921. John A. Macready, pilot. Troy, Ohio

1921 RECEIVED THE MACKAY TROPHY
First time

1922 ENDURANCE RECORD FLIGHT
San Diego, CA. 35 hrs., 18 min.

1922 WORLD RECORD ENDURANCE FLIGHT
April 22, 1922. Dayton, Ohio. 36 hrs., 4 min., 34 sec.

1922 RECEIVED THE MACKAY TROPHY
Second time

1923 FIRST NON-STOP TRANSCONTINENTAL FLIGHT
Across the U.S., May 2-3, 1923, N.Y.-San Diego

1923 FIRST PHOTOGRAPHS, SOLAR ECLIPSE
At 16,000 feet altitude over San Diego, California

1923 FIRST AERIAL PHOTOGRAPHIC EXPEDITION OF AMERICA

1923 FIRST AND ONLY MAN TO RECEIVE THE MACKAY TROPHY THREE TIMES

1924 FIRST NIGHT PARACHUTE JUMP
June 20, 1924 from a burning plane over Dayton, Ohio

1924 FIRST HIGH ALTITUDE PHOTOGRAPHY
Photographed at 32,220 feet over Dayton, Ohio

Introduction

*M*AY 2, 1998 COMMEMORATED THE 75th anniversary of the first non-stop transcontinental flight. *John Macready — Aviation Pioneer* has been written to celebrate that far-reaching achievement and the man who made it happen.

On May 2, 1923, John Macready and his partner Oakley Kelly skipped off the runway at Long Island's Roosevelt Field in an overloaded Fokker T-2 Transport and landed, 27 hours later, at North Island in San Diego.

During the 1920s, aviation was unsophisticated and dangerous.

Pilots who took to the skies risked their lives to the whims of nature, the laws of physics, and the temperaments of untested machines. Nevertheless, a group of daring young aviators with the United States Army Air Service at McCook Field in Dayton, Ohio, dedicated themselves to taming the wild beast of flight and helped to make air travel the essential aspect of American life that we know today.

None of these aeronautic pioneers accomplished more in such a short time than John Macready, the chief test pilot for the Air Service from 1920 to 1926. This shy, yet brave, pilot with a movie star's good looks spent six years in the sky testing the limits of manned flight.

John Macready . . .

- made the first non-stop flight across the United States
- was the first to fly above 35,000 feet (in an open-cockpit biplane!)
- invented the first aviator glasses
- took the first photographs of a solar eclipse
- made the first night parachute jump
- made the first aerial photographic survey of America
- was the world's first crop-duster
- conducted the first tests in a pressurized cockpit
- was the first and only person to win the Mackay Trophy for achievement in aviation three times

During my childhood, legendary aviators such as Orville Wright, Jimmy Doolittle, and Charles Lindbergh frequently dropped by our house to visit my father. Our home was filled with stories of heroic achievements, and my father's mingled easily with the rest. But after becoming a pilot myself, I came to realize just how unique and significant were my father's aviation accomplishments. In 1972, I finally sat him down to tell me his life's story. This book celebrates that remarkable life.

. . . The heavily laden plane covered almost a mile at 110 mph — its top speed — yet still was not airborne. As the pilots raced toward the end of the runway, with the plane's tires still spinning through the grass, Kelly, who could see a disastrous crash staring him in the face, throttled back and aborted the takeoff.

Chapter 1

Coast-to-Coast, Hour Zero

The First Attempt to Leave Roosevelt Field, New York
ON WEDNESDAY, MAY 2, 1923, John A. "Mac" Macready, the United States Army Air Service's dashing, young, chief test pilot, and his partner, Oakley G. Kelly, walked across the grass runway at Long Island's Roosevelt Field toward their modified Fokker T-2 Transport. Once inside the huge monoplane, which sat gleaming in the afternoon sunlight with its nose to the wind, its Liberty engine roaring, and its exhaust stack smoking, they prepared to lift off into the sky above and to become the first men to fly non-stop across the United States from coast-to-coast.

The two fliers had spent the weekend bent over Weather Bureau maps looking for evidence of a "Hudson Bay High," a condition in which the prevailing winds reverse themselves and blow from east to west. One such weather system had already passed through the region and a second was in progress, leading forecasters to warn the two eager pilots that the chances were slim of a third one coming through in the same year. However, on Monday, a small, seemingly insignificant high-pressure area appeared in the southwestern portion of Canada, which they watched with considerable interest. With only one reporting station near the Hudson Bay, area weather conditions were difficult to follow. As the reports came in, Mac and Kelly grew increasingly restless.

By Tuesday morning, the Canadian high pressure area had grown, and a storm or low-pressure area, which had been approaching the Mid-Atlantic region, appeared to have changed course, indicating that the spreading high was forcing the low farther south. That was good news for the two pilots, who immediately began making their last-minute preparations.

On Wednesday morning, Mac and Kelly received a telegram informing them that low clouds and rain awaited them from Dayton all the way through Missouri. Although trying to fly over Missouri's Ozark Mountains in the middle of a rainstorm struck them as a hazardous adventure to be avoided, they decided to leave. Where the sky was clear they would have a full moon above them. Besides, that day would offer them their last chance to make the journey for another year.

The pilots had arrived at the field before dawn to prepare for the flight. Following the tradition of their previous attempts, Kelly took the helm for takeoff. Mac, who was the senior airman, would pilot the landing.

Kelly checked the controls, waved to the small crowd that had gathered for the occasion, and then put the plane in motion at 5:50 a.m.

The T-2 was the U.S. Army Air Service's pioneer monoplane passenger carrier, loaded down that day with 10,850 pounds of fuel in added tanks. With high wings spanning 80 feet, it was the world's largest passenger plane, and was powered by a 400-hp Liberty-12 single engine.

That early Wednesday morning, the heavily laden plane covered almost a mile at 110 mph — its top speed — yet still was not airborne. As the pilots raced toward the end of the runway, with the plane's tires still spinning through the grass, Kelly, who could see a disastrous crash staring him in the face, throttled back and aborted the takeoff.

◈

Beginnings — The Early Years in Searchlight, Nevada

Mac first flew when he was five years old. It was a short flight, and, in truth, he fell rather than flew. He had been happily walking along the top of a high brick wall when, much to his surprise, he lost his balance and tumbled onto the concrete sidewalk below. After recovering from the shock, he succumbed to the natural instincts of a five-year-old and burst into tears. But good Scotsmen don't cry, his father, Benjamin, scolded him. They scream, shout, and sometimes curse, but they never cry. His father's lesson, of which Mac would be reminded many times throughout his childhood, was one he always remembered.

◈

Mac was born in San Diego, California, on October 14, 1887. He and his family moved to the Los Angeles area where Benjamin became managing editor of a local newspaper. The Macreadys lived on Berenda Street in the Pico Heights section, which, in the late 1800s, had all the characteristics of the remote countryside. Once every morning, a horse-drawn streetcar carried the locals to town, and in the evening, it returned to Pico Heights. If you missed its arrival, you walked or stayed home.

Mac attended the Berenda School, a short walk from home. The building was small, so several grades shared a single classroom. The teachers, who believed in the old adage "spare the rod and spoil the child," meted out swift discipline to all deserving students, ensuring that they had no spoiled children.

As a self-described "shrimp," Mac often found himself bullied by the larger schoolboys. Unwilling to accept such treatment, he fought anyone who would accept his challenge. Once, when he had decided to teach a lesson to a particularly annoying bully named Johnny Maltman, he found himself at the receiving end of Maltman's windmill punches. Before Mac could defend himself, he fell to the ground bruised and bloody. That he had fallen before a crowd of his peers made his defeat especially humiliating.

When his mother, Mattie — a woman as tough as her rugged husband — saw how her son had been beaten, she walked him down to the Van Duzer School of Boxing where she enrolled him in a course in proper fisticuffs. Mac worked hard in the gym and in the school yard, and within a short time learned to use his fists with damaging precision. Many years later, while a student at Stanford University, he won the West Coast Golden Gloves Championship. By then, of course, bullies like Johnny Maltman had moved on to easier challenges.

When Mac was still young, Benjamin Macready, who had an adventurous spirit, succumbed to "gold fever," quit the newspaper business, and plunged with vigor into mining. But because the desert was no place for a family, he left Mac, his two other sons, and his wife in Los Angeles. Mac watched quietly as his father loaded cartons, boxes, and trunks into the buckboard and set out for Searchlight, Nevada, a lawless camp in the southwest corner of the state where gunfights over claim-jumping, women, or gambling were everyday occurrences and where numerous odd characters made their home — like Sam. Yet, the craggy camp cook, who, after inheriting the New Era Mine as compensation for past wages, became one of the town's richest men. In 1906, at the height of Searchlight's glory, 35 saloons splashed whiskey over the counters to thirsty miners and some 10,000 people milled up and down Main Street's wooden sidewalks.

Along with his partners, Mr. Fisher and Mr. Hubbard, Ben staked out his claim and enthusiastically prospected for gold. The three men doggedly followed veins with pickaxes and shovels — their days turning into weeks, their weeks turning into months — without finding their strike. Each night they returned to camp tired, dirty, lonely, and frustrated.

Then, one day, Ben found something amid the sand and gravel while panning in a gulch just below the claim of a man named Jim Swickard. Turning his pan under the sun, he recognized the unmistakable glitter of gold, and his spirits leaped. He picked out some with his finger and examined it closely. It surely looked like the real thing!

Jim Swickard was a big, heavy, well-meaning man whose strength was in his muscle, not his intellect. Ben guessed that if what he had found was real gold, it had probably come from Swickard's claim, which, until then, had been thought to contain nothing more than a worthless copper vein among the green ore. But Ben decided against sharing the news with

Swickard. Instead, he picked up his pan and hurried back to tell his partners about his discovery.

"Look here. Look right down there. What do you see?" he asked, while showing Hubbard and Fisher his pan.

"Looks like gold. Real gold," Hubbard replied. "Where'd you find it?"

Ben explained his theory about how the gold had come from Swickard's claim, and together they tried to work up a plan for getting the rights before their neighbor discovered the gold himself. As they knew, Swickard had little faith in the honesty of other miners, having posted signs all over his property that, when translated for politeness, read: "Any sheep-herding sons of guns who I catch digging on these here claims will get new buttonholes in their pockmarked skins." So to avoid being shot, they disregarded the thought of digging without permission and decided on a straightforward approach.

The three partners found Swickard and offered to buy his claim. But he refused. So, after engaging him in casual conversation, Ben asked, "I say, Jim, you've been out here on the desert for a long time now. If you could have anything you wanted, right this minute, what would it be? What's your heart's desire; what do you want more than anything in the world?"

Swickard thought for a moment, staring at the ground. Then he looked up and said earnestly, "What I'd really like more than anything is a fine team of mules and the best camping outfit money can buy. That's what I'd really like."

The three partners rushed into San Bernardino to purchase a team of mules and a camping outfit. When they had concluded their business, they returned to the claim site. After pulling in alongside Swickard's camp, announcing their arrival with a loud "whoa there, whoa" and a snap of the whip, they proceeded to set up their fancy new equipment while noting with satisfaction the look of extreme envy on Swickard's face. When Swickard could no longer suppress his curiosity, he sauntered over to the Macready-Fisher-Hubbard campsite, and with poorly conjured casualness queried, "What you got there, fellows?"

"What do you mean?" asked Ben, feigning innocence.

"That's a mighty fine team of mules and camp outfit. Where'd you get it?"

"Just got back from town with it," Ben replied. "Finest team anywhere around, they said."

"You wouldn't consider selling it, would you?"

For $1,100, the team of mules, and the camping outfit, Swickard wrote out a quitclaim deed in longhand. The next morning he hitched the mules to his wagon and headed south, happy with his good fortune.

The ecstatic partners quickly wrote out an agreement providing all three equal share in any profits from the newly acquired claim. Then they set out to work the location where Ben had found the gold-bearing ore. They hacked at rocks with picks, dug out the chunks with shovels, sifted through the gravel in their pans, and threw out the worthless stuff, only to start all over again. But after months of back-breaking effort, they had found no gold. They even began to suspect that Swickard had tricked them, rather than the other way around.

Finally discouraged and tired of working in the hot desert sun without any success, Hubbard and Fisher quit. They left for Los Angeles, claiming that they were giving up the mining business altogether, leaving Ben alone in Nevada.

Determined not to give up, Ben continued working with undiminished zeal. Each day he awoke knowing that this would be the day he would strike his gold-bearing vein. The work was tough and lonely, but, coming from sturdy Scottish stock, he refused to stop trying. The death-like stillness of the desert was the hardest to take; men had gone crazy after suffering through months with no sounds other than the occasional howl of a coyote, the cry of a bobcat, or the hoot of an owl at night. He worked, slept, and ate alone.

Then one day when he had moved to a new spot considerably lower than the original finding, Ben was picking at some ore he had previously failed to notice. Crumbling it up, he put it in the pan, added water, swished the gravel around, and recognized that unmistakable glint. He tried to contain his excitement. After all, who knew if it was a real vein? His last finding had led to nothing. He dug deeper into the outcropping and found even larger chunks. Several more exploratory hacks with the pickax confirmed his suspicions; the vein, which was buried in quartz, looked big — so big that he would need help mining it. He set off for the assayer's office with a few nuggets, after carefully covering over his diggings and leaving a staked-claim sign. He had the deeds in his pocket; the gold was his!

The vein proved to be too rich for one man to work alone, so Ben sought backing from a Boston financier named Colonel C. W. Hopkins, who had come out West at the request of Fred Dunn, another miner. Eager to invest in the mining business, Hopkins forwarded Ben $5,000, and together they formed The Quartette District, as the mine was later named. Ben used the money to sink a shaft to approximately 300 feet, but found nothing.

Fearing that he would lose his entire investment, Hopkins sent a message to Dunn, his representative at the mine, instructing him to inform Ben that he refused to advance any more money. But Ben was in Los Angeles at the time. So Dunn told the foreman, Jack Russell, to close down the mine. Russell, who had never met Dunn before, responded that he only took orders from Benjamin Macready and continued his work. Without telling Russell, he also sent a wire to Ben that explained the situation.

Ben returned Russell's wire with a message consisting of only two words: "Crosscut south."

Following Ben's instructions, Russell and his team found the ore shoot and, passing through ten feet of "$40 rock," reached the hanging wall. From that time onward, the Quartette Mine was a record producer, eventually maintaining tunnels under 102 acres and producing $3.5 million in gold-oxide ore.

When word of the profitable Quartette mine reached Los Angeles, Ben's former partners, Hubbard and Fisher, showed up on the Macready doorstep with opened palms. That they would want two-thirds of the wealth, which Ben's hard work had produced, struck him as ridiculous. But when the matter went to court, he was forced to share the profits, because Hubbard and Fisher had left Nevada without signing over their rights to him.

The Quartette mine attracted fortune seekers to Searchlight and helped create a boom town in the middle of the desert. Ben eventually acquired interests in the Santa Fe, St. Louis, Quaker Girl Group, Bishop, and Saturn mines. And, as his prominence in the town grew, he was elected Justice of the Peace. Mac later recalled that many of the children born in Searchlight during the first decade of the 20th century were named Macready after his father.

When Mac turned 12, his father sent him and his brothers to spend the summer working in the mines. Ben firmly believed that his boys should "get out early and rustle for themselves." So the three young men were soon working alongside the grizzled old miners, many of whom, as immigrants, knew no English. Ben insisted that his boys should be treated just as any other worker was and disallowed his foreman to show them any favoritism.

The Macready boys took the train from Los Angeles to where the line ended in Goffs, California, spent the night in an overpriced and smelly bunkhouse, and then took the six-horse stagecoach to Searchlight. The driver was a skilled horseman and also a drunk, who made the trip especially exciting for three boys out on their own. When he reached the edge of Searchlight, he would gather the reins together and excite his team with a wild yell, "Hyah there! Giddya up!" He cracked the whip, and the horses bolted straight down Main Street — scattering dogs, children, and anyone else unfortunate enough to be in the way and kicking up a terrific cloud of dust as the coach came to a dramatic stop in front of Kirk Burdick's Wellington Saloon.

All the town's characters hung out in front of the Wellington, chewing tobacco, shooting the breeze, or "just a-sittin'." The men gathered there to watch the cowboys who had come to town on Saturday night, loaded with cash and booze, to raise a little hell and find some women. On dull days, to stir up a bit of excitement, prospectors squared off two tough jackasses and watched them gnash their teeth and kick up their heels at each other. They waged thousands of dollars and, occasionally, a mining claim on the outcome of those burro fights.

Eating at the Quartette mess, a three-mile walk through the blistering heat, was a study in survival. Fortunately for young Mac, his friendship with a burly miner named Vince saved him from starvation. When the cook announced dinner by ringing his triangle, a mob scene ensued as all the hungry men raced for the long wooden tables laden with mounds of food. Vince, who was the biggest man around, would plunk himself down in the center of the bench, squeeze Mac in beside him, then start dragging platters toward himself with both hands. After heaping his plate high, he would pass a platter on to Mac and say gruffly, "You better get yours while it's here, boy." As long as Mac could squeeze in beside Vince, he ate well.

True to his Scottish heritage, Ben was sparing with a dollar, yet he gladly paid for his sons' education. When, Mac reached college age in 1907, his father sent him off to Stanford University where his older brother

George had studied. Although Ben paid for Mac's tuition, room, and board, Mac had to provide his own spending money. Therefore, working the mines during the summers became essential.

When Mac graduated from Stanford in 1912, with a degree in economics, he had planned to enter the investment business in Los Angeles. But before heading south, he stopped in Searchlight where his parents had asked him to look after the house until they returned from a trip to Canada. His "short visit" lasted four years and postponed his investment career indefinitely.

By the time of Mac's arrival, Searchlight had become a relatively lawless town. Its citizenry, having grown increasingly frustrated with the situation, began looking for someone to uphold the law who was honest, fair, intelligent, and trustworthy. During Mac's youth, Mattie had forbidden the consumption of alcohol in her home — because her father had been a heavy drinker — so, consequently, Mac abstained from liquor. He had been a hard-working regular in the mines since the age of 12 and had never asked for any special treatment. The miners, who were drunk much of the time, liked and respected him. And as a college graduate and the son of one of the town's most prominent founders, he fit the job description better than anyone else around. In 1913, Searchlight elected the 25-year-old John Macready their new Justice of the Peace.

Mac's first test as a lawman came soon after he took office. The husky, tough, and slow-witted town bully, Jue Martin, had made a reputation for himself roughing up the men who hung around the Wellington. When Martin learned of Mac's reputation as a boxer, he bragged to anyone who would listen that he "could beat anybody around, including the new JP." Although Mac was half Martin's size, the town encouraged him to teach the thug a lesson. To defend his honor and reputation, Mac agreed to a fight.

Their battle quickly became the talk in Searchlight's thirteen saloons and the two grocery stores. Although the official odds favored Mac — more from a desire by the locals to see him win than from their conviction that he would — many timorous souls hedged their bets by putting money on both men.

As the noon hour approached on the appointed day, the crowd gathered at the Wellington, milling about, making last-minute wagers. By the time Mac entered the saloon, Martin was busy throwing punches at invisible targets, kicking up dust with his footwork, and expounding his usual braggadocio. "I'll knock his head off first punch I land. He won't even know what hit him. You just watch!" he proclaimed.

Mac walked quietly through the swinging doors and removed his shirt and undershirt; Martin followed suit. The two men positioned themselves ten feet apart, facing each other with fists at the ready, while Kirk Burdick, the self-appointed referee, gave the terse instructions: "Get in there and fight. Last one standing wins." With that, he blew the whistle, and the fight began.

Mac knew that if Martin ever landed a punch, he was through — wiped out. His only hope of survival was to stay out of Martin's reach until he could land a solid punch of his own.

As Martin came at him swinging hard, jabbing with his right, hooking with his left, Mac ducked and swayed, circling around his opponent. The more Martin missed, the harder he swung and the more frustrated and angry he became. Mac continued dodging and ducking away from Martin's terrifying fists, landing a jab whenever Martin lost his balance from a wild swing. As the fight continued and the day's heat grew increasingly oppressive inside the stuffy room, Martin's history of attendance at the town's saloons quickly began to weigh him down. He huffed and wheezed, moving more slowly and throwing weaker, less accurate punches.

Mac saw his chance and threw a hard right at Martin's momentarily exposed jaw. The punch landed with precision, knocking Martin out cold and, to the horror of all the spectators, popping one of his eyeballs from its socket. The eyeball bounced across the floor, making a trail through the dirt until it rolled to a stop at Mac's feet. Bending over to get a closer look, Mac discovered the best-kept secret in Searchlight — Jue Martin, the town bully, had a glass eye.

Mac's job as Justice of the Peace paid poorly, so he continued working in the mines when his legal duties allowed. Most of the time the sparsely populated town was quiet. Twenty store-front buildings lined the one main thoroughfare, and dusty trails led haphazardly from Main Street into the desert toward mining camps and distant communities. A 20-mule team passed through town every other day hauling produce and other commodities to the outlying camps.

When the town constable, Tom Connell, made an arrest for wife-beating, fighting, murder, prostitution, or some other typical crime, he notified Mac, who would set a time and date for a trial. On the appointed day, the Searchlight Bench and Bar convened in the old abandoned newspaper building owned by Mac's father Ben. Lawyers came from all over Arizona, Nevada, and Southern California to represent their clients, most often in land disputes. Resplendent and dignified in his black frock coat and tie, Mac would climb up on the dais, stand before his chair, and declare, "The court is now in session."

Although Mac had a good sense of right and wrong, he was short on legal training, and so he relied heavily on his imposing volume of the *Statutes of the State of Nevada*. Hoping to capitalize on the judge's legal naïveté, visiting lawyers would try to intimidate him by burying their arguments in a mountain of terminology and technicalities. Never ruffled by such tactics, Mac would instruct them to restate their case in simple terms, setting forth the pertinent facts.

R. H. Cabell, a tall, aristocratic lawyer from Virginia, who was always nattily dressed in a morning coat, striped trousers, and spats, came before Mac to argue a tricky property case. Casually citing whole paragraphs and sections from the *Statutes,* he rambled on without pause until Mac, who had been listening in respectful silence, interrupted him. "Now just a minute, Mr. Cabell. Would you mind pointing out that last statute for me please. Show me exactly where it is in the book so I can see it."

Cabell approached the bench and started thumbing through the heavy book, running his long tapered forefinger along the margins. When he failed to find what he was looking for, he repeated his search from the beginning. Mac allowed him to thumb through the book until he realized that the lawyer was stalling. Nevada had no such statute.

"Case dismissed," Mac said, banging down his gavel.

Sometimes being a Justice of the Peace in a small town meant that Mac was forced to judge his friends. One night Constable Connell, Mac's coworker and close friend, was arrested and jailed for beating his wife. Barrel-chested and strong as an ox, Connell was a popular figure in the mines and along Searchlight's Main Street, so everyone expected the trial to be biased in his favor. On the day of the hearing, Connell walked confidently into the courtroom and stood before Judge Macready while the testimony was read. Connell had beaten his wife so seriously that she was confined to her bed.

Mac listened carefully to the testimony of witnesses and the arresting officer, knowing that no one in Searchlight would blame him for going light on the defendant. But he refused to set a bad precedent. So, banging his gavel and looking straight at the accused, he confidently pronounced the verdict: "Guilty as charged. Thirty days in the county jail for the defendant, Tom Connell."

Connell was stunned. Thirty days! As his deputies hauled him off to jail, he announced to everyone within earshot that when his 30 days were over, he would "get Macready."

Mac was anxious about running into the constable at the end of the 30-day period, but when he eventually came upon Connell waiting beside the mine shaft, Mac continued toward him without missing a step, greeting him with a "Good morning, Tom."

Connell hesitated for a second, then returned the greeting. "Good morning, John." Wearing a wide grin, he held out his hand, and the two men shook.

"No hard feelings, Tom?" Mac asked.

"No hard feelings," Connell answered. "Actually, you did me a good turn putting me away like that. I had a lot of time to think while I was in that jail. First, I was so angry I could have killed you, but then I began to realize it was just what I had coming to me. I'd been getting away with beating her up for a long time, but no one ever had the courage to do anything about it before. I gotta hand it to you."

The two men put their arms around each other's shoulders and descended into the shaft, closer friends for their legal confrontation.

As Justice of the Peace, Mac performed many of the town's weddings and certified many of its deaths. He conducted the brief wedding services in a tradition that had been handed down to him by his predecessor, John Wheatley: "Stand up, join hands, in the name of John Wheatley and Jesus Christ I now pronounce you man and wife. That will be two dollars and fifty cents, please." His mother, Mattie, held receptions at the Macready family home, because she felt the local hotels and saloons were inappropriate for such festivities.

Mac assumed his role as coroner whenever a citizen of Searchlight passed away, which most often resulted from a mining accident. One day a miner came riding at full gallop into town, flung himself off his horse in front of the Wellington, and yelled, "Where's the doc? We've got a real bad accident out at El Dorado Canyon." As an afterthought he added, "Better get the Judge, too. We may need him if the doc can't help."

When Mac and Doc McIntyre arrived in the buckboard, they learned that a miner who had lit a blast at the bottom of the shaft had been caught in the explosion. What was left of the man had been brought to the surface and laid out on a blanket. Although he was still conscious, his body was a mass of bone and bloody, torn flesh. His arms, legs, and much of his face had been blown apart. He was still in shock, so the pain had not yet reached him.

The doctor hesitated before going for his black bag. He knew that the miner would never survive the 35-mile trip to Las Vegas or the excruciating pain when he recovered from his shock. Yet as a physician, he had taken an oath never to harm anyone. He took a hypodermic needle out of his bag, filled it from a vial that he kept in his pocket, and, bending over the miner, thrust the needle into the broken body. Straightening, he said to the foreman, "You can lift him carefully onto the buckboard now. We'll take him back to town. I gave him something to ease the pain. When he comes to, he won't feel anything."

As he and Mac rode back to town, Dr. McIntyre confessed that he had compassionately put the poor miner out of his misery and asked Mac never to reveal his secret. The miner was buried the next morning — desert burials couldn't wait — and Mac kept the doctor's confidence.

Mac had lived in Searchlight just over a year when he met Jim Cashman. The two men became close friends and, eventually, business partners. When Mac's parents left for a trip to Europe in early 1918, Mac became superintendent of his father's Santa Fe Mining Company. The mine owners were having trouble shipping their ore to the mill, because Nevada had no reliable shippers or freight lines, so Mac and Cashman decided to organize their own shipping company. They bought a good four-horse team and a flat-bottomed wagon. Then they obtained contracts from the various mine owners to haul their ore to the Southern Nevada Mill, which, incidentally, was owned by Ben Macready. The young Justice of the Peace, walking alongside his team and fully loaded ore wagon soon became a familiar sight.

The Cashman-Macready partnership next acquired a rundown inoperable ferry, which the two men proceeded to renovate and repair. In better days, the Aravada Ferry, as it had been known, had operated on the Colorado River between Arizona and Nevada. The partners soon had it hauling automobiles, people, freight, and horses and wagons across the river.

Then, seeing a need for transportation from Searchlight to the river crossing, the enterprising young men bought horses and a stagecoach and set up a stage line between the town and Chloride, Arizona, providing some sorely needed transportation for travelers between the two points, and some cash for themselves. Before long, they established a stagecoach link connecting the Arrowhead Trail at Searchlight and the Old Trails Road at Kingman, Arizona, considerably shortening the travel time between the two mining towns.

With these business ventures, Mac and his partner had provided much-needed transportation links from the town to the outside world.

In 1915, Mac entered politics and was elected to membership in the Clark County Republican Central Committee. As his businesses prospered and more stages and wagons were added, the number of passengers and the amount of freight increased.

At about this time, Mac branched out into the cattle business. His partner in this venture was Clark Parker, an experienced cattleman whose job was to acquire cattle while Mac developed the watering holes. Experienced in the art of locating water on the barren desert, Mac dug out the holes and installed pipes and troughs. Parker knew that cattle ranged near water and used this tendency to "acquire" new animals, as Mac found out later. Range land was open and uninterrupted by fences, and when some of the 3,000 head that belonged to the Rock Springs Land and Cattle Company — a merger of area ranchers — gathered around Mac's watering holes, Parker roped any unbranded cows or calves, put his brand on them, and turned them loose with his herd.

By 1916, young John Macready had become one of Searchlight's most prominent citizens — the son of town-founder Benjamin Macready, a successful businessman, a significant local politician. He was reelected Searchlight's Justice of the Peace and continued to live and prosper there until World War I changed the direction of his life.

Many years later, Mac was flying a new and fast experimental airplane built by Keith Ryder, of Los Angeles, in the Chicago Air Races. Halfway through the race, the aircraft developed such a bad case of wing flutter that the wings shook apart. He managed to glide what remained of the fuselage away from the crowd of spectators, crashing in a field nearby. The plane smashed to pieces upon impact — no single piece was found over a foot long. Although having just broken almost every bone in his body, he remained conscious and heard a voice come from the crowd that had gathered around him.

"He's alive! I know he is! You can't kill the Sheriff of Searchlight, Nevada!" someone shouted.

. . . As Macready and Kelly headed out across the great expanse of America on what would become a 2,500-mile journey, they crossed their fingers and hoped their compass was accurate.

Chapter 2

Coast-to-Coast, Hour One

Takeoff from Roosevelt Field

AS OAKLEY KELLY TAXIED THE T-2 back to its starting position, Mac remembered the suggestion of a 17-year-old Roosevelt Field mechanic named Carl "Slim" Hennick that they begin their takeoff 200 or 300 feet back on ground that he knew was safe.

Roosevelt Field, at Westbury, Long Island, New York — now the site of Roosevelt Raceway and a shopping mall — was a one-mile-square plateau that sat 20 feet above the adjacent Hazelhurst Field. At the far end of Hazelhurst stood a row of airmail hangars. When an aircraft took off from Roosevelt, its nose pointed directly at those hangars, and Hennick thought that with the extra room, the T-2 might have a better chance to clear the structures. Grateful for the advice, Mac made the recommendation to Kelly, who steered the monoplane farther out into the field.

As the pilots waved good-bye to the small group of anxious spectators, Air Service Colonel Franklin R. Kenney overheard a man proclaim, "What fools those boys are. They'll never make it."

The T-2 lumbered heavily across the bumpy field, bouncing but refusing to rise. Colonel Kenney bristled.

"I'll bet you $5,000 even-money they will!"

The T-2's wheels were still rolling along the ground when it ran out of room. "I wonder what's going to happen when we hit that drop-off," Mac wondered. His curiosity was quickly satisfied, because they flopped over the edge of the runway and disappeared from sight.

The crowd ran to pick up the pieces of the ruined aircraft, but when they arrived, they discovered that Mac and Kelly had miraculously survived the drop and were flying just a few feet off the ground — so low they could "reach out and pick the daisies."

With the Hazelhurst hangars looming in the distance, Kelly pulled back on the stick to make the T-2 rise, but it resisted his efforts and led them straight toward disaster. Just in time — possibly because of luck, divine intervention, or sheer will power — the plane lifted itself to a height where it could barely clear the hangar roofs. Later, Mac admitted that he didn't know whether they would get over them. "We both expected to hit those hangars."

Although the Liberty engine was wide open, the aircraft rose by inches instead of feet. A single misfire of a cylinder would have sent the T-2 barreling into fences, telephone wires, and farmhouses. "We could only gain a few hundred feet altitude, no matter how we stalled the plane to climb," Kelly commented later.

By the time they had reached Coney Island, some 22 miles to the west/southwest, they had only gained 300 feet of altitude, and no amount of maneuvering could coax the plane higher. Over Pennsylvania, some 65 to 70 miles westward, they finally picked up another 100 feet, but Kelly began to worry about their course because the rivers, roads, and railways below wound in every direction and smoke from the cities blotted out important landmarks. In the West, even in uninhabited areas, section lines laid out decades before by surveyors or homesteaders stretched north and south or east and west so accurately that aviators used them to check their compasses. But Pennsylvania had been settled earlier and more haphazardly, which offered them no help in finding their way.

As Macready and Kelly headed out across the great expanse of America on what would become a 2,500-mile journey, they crossed their fingers and hoped their compass was accurate.

⨭

Up, Up, and Away —
Flight Training at Rockwell, Gerstner, and Brooks Fields

News of the war in Europe had reached the Nevada desert slowly and sporadically. At first, no one paid much attention because the conflict seemed too distant and unreal to understand. Gradually the rumblings grew louder, the talk became more militant, and the U.S. entered World War I.

One day in May 1917, a recruiting sergeant arrived in Searchlight. As he stepped off the stagecoach with his briefcase and valise, he looked to be prepared to stay awhile. He walked to a rooming house near the Yellowstone Saloon to arrange for his lodging, then went across the street to the lobby of the Kennedy House Hotel where he set up his desk.

Mac had been brought up in a home full of fierce patriotism. His maternal grandmother, Ma Beck, who wielded considerable authority within the family, had firm ideas about a young man's duty to his country. When America entered a war, you volunteered and served. If you failed to do so, you would be a disgrace to your family and your country. The matter was that simple. Partly due to Ma's influence, Mac was one of the first men in Searchlight to sign up with the recruiting sergeant. For lack of a better choice, he enlisted in the U.S. Cavalry.

"Just fill out these enlistment papers right here," the sergeant directed. "You'll have to go to Reno to be sworn in. I'll give you a note for the lieutenant up there, and he'll take care of the details."

The papers signed, Mac went off to arrange his affairs. Not knowing when he might return, he disposed of his freight-hauling interests, resigned his civic office, and quit the mining business.

During the early part of the 20th century, no roads connected Searchlight and Reno, so in order to travel the 509 miles between the two towns

Mac took the stagecoach to Goffs, California, and boarded a train for Los Angeles. There, he transferred to another train to San Francisco, where he took another for the trip to Reno. He paid for every aspect of his journey out of his own pocket.

In an effort to pass the long tedious hours of train travel, Mac read anything he could find. An article in one of the magazines he picked up described a new area of military service — aviation. Still in its formative stages, the U.S. Army Air Service intended to become an elite arm of the U.S. Signal Corps that would accept young men subject to their perfect physical health and their completion of a college education. His interest piqued, Mac grew eager to learn more about this new branch of the service.

Once he had arrived in Reno, Mac found the recruiting lieutenant ensconced in comfortable quarters at the luxurious Riverside Hotel. After giving his name, handing over the sergeant's note, and answering a few preliminary questions, he broached the subject uppermost on his mind. "What's this new branch that's opening up, Sir? I'd like to try for that if it's possible, instead of the Cavalry."

"I really don't know too much about it," the lieutenant answered. "Tell you what I'll do though. I'll write Washington and see what information they can give us. You hang around until I hear back. Might take a little time though. Meanwhile, you can get your physical and be ready for whatever comes through."

The "little time" turned into two weeks, with Mac impatiently cooling his heels on the front porch of the Riverside Hotel — at his own expense.

Finally, word arrived. "I have Washington's approval here for you to transfer to the aviation section of the Signal Corps," the lieutenant said, handing Mac the letter. "You passed the physical, you have a college degree, so you qualified, and your application was approved. I'll swear you right in and you can leave for Berkeley today."

Mac was elated.

❧

Nestled in the Berkeley hills overlooking the San Francisco Bay, the University of California was home to the School of Military Aeronautics, where, along with the other aviation section cadets, Mac trained to fly without setting foot in an aircraft. Primarily, he practiced coming to

muster, and close-order drills, and learned some of the finer points of flying: "You push the stick forward to descend, pull it back to climb, shove
it to the left to turn left, and to the right to turn right." He and the other
cadets slept on a bare floor in their bedrolls.

One of Mac's roommates at Berkeley was Corliss C. Moseley, who later
won the 1920 Pulitzer Trophy in the 600-hp, 156 mph, VCP-R (Racer)
Verville-Packard biplane at Mitchell Field, Long Island. Their paths
crossed many times during the next few years, and Moseley and his wife
eventually became frequent houseguests of the Macreadys in Dayton,
Ohio, after both men were married. Waldo Waterman, who later became a
familiar name in aviation circles, was one of the instructors.

As a cadet in training, Mac was officially a private making $31 a month.
At that salary, he would need many months to recoup what he had spent
trying to transfer to the Signal Corps.

After several months of pre-flight training at Berkeley, Mac and his fellow cadets moved to Rockwell Field, San Diego, where they became
acquainted with the ubiquitous Curtiss JN-4 "Jenny" trainer. Mac's assignment at Rockwell lasted from August through December 1917 — a lovely
season in San Diego, yet a difficult one for the young cadet.

The entire flying field and runway at Rockwell Field consisted of one
big cow pasture liberally sprinkled with sagebrush and jackrabbit holes.
During landings, the pilots took their toll of the scampering jackrabbits
crossing the runway, and the jackrabbit holes and sagebrush clumps, like-
wise, took their toll of pilots and planes.

The Jenny, powered by a 90-hp Curtiss OX-5 engine generating 75
mph, was one of the earliest mass-produced American aircraft and was
used primarily for training. But those famous old biplanes, on which the
first aviators cut their teeth, were "bad news." They defied balance, took
off wrong, and flew funny when aloft. Later models proved to be reliable
and trustworthy, but the early Jenny trainers drove the cadets crazy. Landing one was a nightmare. The biplane had rubber shock absorber cords for
landing gear, so when the wheels touched down on the runway, the aircraft
bounced like a rubber ball. The inexperienced cadets scrunched wings,
bent propellers and landing gear, and demolished entire planes. Sometimes the pilots walked away; other times they weren't so lucky.

Colonel Dade, the commanding officer of the field, was not a pilot, but
a former Cavalry officer who looked every inch the part, from his long,
drooping mustache, his splay-hipped riding jodhpurs held up by a regula-

tion Sam Brown belt, and his shiny officer's sword, to his high, brown, well-worn, spur-wrapped boots. Flying was still in its infancy, so the military had few fliers and even fewer instructors. Like Dade, those who wrote the new aviation regulations based their understanding of manned flight on their understanding of horseback riding: "Spurs were to be removed before mounting the plane."

Colonel Dade obviously had little patience for the peculiarities of aviation. One morning while Mac was in the colonel's office, Dade called for his adjutant. Walking briskly up to his superior's desk, the young captain clicked his heels together smartly, gave a snappy salute, and, standing at attention, said, "Yes, Sir!" Dade, who had been looking over some reports, peered up from the stack of papers and asked, "What's this all about? What's the reason for all these smashed up planes?"

"Those are due to bad landings, Sir," the adjutant answered.

"Well!" barked Dade. "I'll take care of that. Take a memo, Captain, and see that it gets circulated to every pilot on the base. From now on, there will be no more bad landings on this field."

An oft-repeated story among cadets demonstrates the novelty of early flight. A man taking his first ride in an aircraft sat in the rear cockpit, clinging tightly to its sides, as it rolled and wallowed around in the air. Finally, he could stand it no longer. Reaching forward, he tapped the pilot on the shoulder and asked, "I say, old man, this is my first flight. Couldn't you ease up a bit?"

"You've got nothing on me," the pilot reportedly answered. "This is my second."

The half-dozen hard-boiled, no-nonsense early flight instructors were mostly civilians. One of them, Doc Wildman, who later would be Mac's roommate in Italy during World War II, became the president of the San Diego Chamber of Commerce after the war. Wildman summed up his opinion of the new crop of young would-be fliers in the phrase, "Those damn cadets!" When deciding whether to fly on a given day, he held up his handkerchief and, if it blew away, declared, "Can't fly today boys — too rough."

One particular instructor impressed Mac the most. Mild-mannered Dean Smith, one of the few Regular Army pilots on the field, had a very simple, country-like demeanor. He earned the respect of the students and instructors by patiently straightening out problems and simplifying complex questions.

৯৬

Mac took his first instruction from Max Miller. As Miller would climb into the front cockpit, Mac climbed into the rear. Once airborne, Miller made motions with his hands to indicate which maneuvers he wanted Mac to execute, because they had no means of verbal communication. Mac tried to follow his instructor's commands gracefully, but rarely succeeded.

As weeks passed and Mac's training period neared its conclusion, his landings continued to be a series of controlled crashes. The other cadets seemed to learn quickly, but Mac failed to catch on.

One day shortly before graduation, Mac climbed into the cockpit and took off with Miller in his usual position in the front seat. Mac kept his eyes glued to the instrument panel, watching each dial carefully, trying to coordinate his movements: to keep the wings level, to maintain the proper altitude, and to stay on the correct heading. Yet, every one of his turns seemed more like a roller-coaster ride than an airplane flight.

"Well, Macready," Miller said, once they had landed. "I don't think you'll ever be a pilot. But tomorrow I'm going to let you take it around by yourself. If you get by, fine; if you don't, you won't be in flight training any more."

Mac returned to the barracks feeling so low he said he "could have crawled under a snake's belly while wearing a high silk hat." He wanted to fly more than anything else, yet he found himself flunking out.

Dawn and the bugler awoke the cadets the next morning. Temperatures in the low 40s aided in the hastiness of dressing before falling out for muster. The cadets devoured their breakfast — ham, eggs, pancakes, cereal, fruit juice, and strong coffee — before assembling on the flight line for their solos. One after another, the cadets took off in their Jennys. A rumor was going around that if a cadet could bring himself and his aircraft down in one undamaged piece, he would be officially named a pilot and awarded his wings.

As each cadet went through the prescribed maneuvers, Mac's stomach tied itself in knots. He worried that he would be the only one to flunk the solo. "How humiliating!" Until that morning, he had had only eight hours of dual training.

Finally, the moment came for Mac to fly. As he walked toward the Jenny, he told himself that this was his last chance to become a pilot. Taking off was easy, but keeping the biplane level, maintaining altitude through turns, and landing smoothly were difficult. Mac had always fixed his eyes on the instruments, but this time he had to watch for signals from his instructor on the ground. As he scanned the horizon — the ocean to the west, the mountains to the east — he realized that he should have been looking outside the cockpit all along, and not at the instrument panel. "Why didn't I realize this before?" he wondered. "More to the point, why hadn't Max told me?" From that moment, piloting became easier. As Mac put the plane through the simple maneuvers, he knew he'd pass the test after all. He was going to be a pilot!

Max was more surprised than anyone when his student brought the Jenny down with gentle precision. "What happened up there? You really handled that plane as if you knew what you were doing. You looked good, and I'm proud of you, Macready. You flew it like a pro!" The instructor was suddenly delighted with the pupil he had been prepared to wash out.

The two men became close friends thereafter, and when Max was killed a short time later in a plane crash, Mac considered his death a great personal loss. A few days after his first solo flight, Mac earned his wings and his commission as a second lieutenant.

❧

On December 17, 1917, Mac reported to the School for Instructors at Gerstner Field, at Lake Charles, Louisiana, to begin his advanced training. The airfield was a flat, open space surrounded on all sides by alligator-infested swampland. During his first morning at the base while standing at attention with his fellow officers, Mac received his first official order from Major Ocher, Gerstner's commanding officer. Famous for his unorthodox methods of commanding and of teaching young officers to follow orders,

Ocher called Mac over and asked, "Lieutenant Macready, you see that blackbird over there?"

"Yes, Sir."

"And you see this shotgun right here?"

"Yes, Sir."

"Well, I want you to take that shotgun over there and shoot that blackbird."

Mac, who had never fired a gun before, picked up the rifle and pulled the trigger. He missed his target.

Another young would-be instructor at the field, D. G. Richardson, loved to climb his plane as high and fast as it would go, often risking the aircraft and his own life with his fancy maneuvers. One day, he was performing one of his more elaborate aerial shows when Major Ocher walked out on the field. Ocher stood watching until Richardson landed his plane, climbed out, took off his helmet and goggles, and sauntered toward the hangar.

Ocher called him over to where he was standing. "You really seem to enjoy a fast climb," he observed.

"Yes, Sir, I sure do!" Richardson exclaimed.

"Well, that's good, that's very good," the major said, "because you're going to get some more practice in fast-climbing right now. Put your helmet and goggles back on, Richardson."

The lieutenant eagerly complied.

"Now," Ocher directed, pointing to a 500-foot structure on the far side of the field, "you see that big water tower? You get over there on the double and climb to the top just as fast as you can. Run!"

Gerstner Field was chaotic, with students going up alone in aircraft they had never flown before and instructors on the ground giving orders of which they weren't sure. The young instructors-in-training had few rules to follow, and the lack of organization soon led to numerous unnecessary deaths. Dean Smith, who had preceded Mac to Gerstner Field, set about changing the situation. As Smith's military assistant, Mac implemented sometimes unpopular directives.

On April 10, 1918, Mac was ordered to Brooks Field in San Antonio, Texas, at the request of Dean Smith who had once again preceded him. With his transfer, Mac earned a promotion in rank to captain. He had accumulated 269 hours of flying time in his logbook.

The barracks, administration buildings, and hangars at Brooks Field were in various stages of completion, having been hastily thrown together as the field burst into frenzied activity during the war. Both military and civilian pilots, who came from the only two piloting schools in the country — Rockwell Field at San Diego, California, or Mineola Field on Long Island, New York, ended up at Brooks for training as instructors. Like Mac, many talented young officers who were bitten by the flight bug had enlisted in the nascent Air Service, and thus the field boasted top-notch talent in its officer complement: Loring Pickering, formerly the owner-editor of the San Francisco *Call Bulletin*, was the base executive officer; Hartford Powell, the previous editor of *Collier's Magazine* was the base adjutant; Lamar Seligson would later become a U.S. Senator; and Duke Skoning had been an executive at Standard Oil.

Colonel Conger Pratt, a West Point graduate, was the base commander. The officer in charge of flying was Leo Walton, with Dean Smith as his assistant. As he had done at Gerstner Field, Mac served as Smith's assistant.

Mac later became the officer in charge of flying. In his new position, he oversaw the flight operations of all the different units stationed at the base. He covered the distances easily and quickly by riding in a motorcycle sidecar. Then, the Air Service provided him with a more luxurious means of transportation: a Cadillac limousine, complete with driver. The car proved useful socially, because young ladies from San Antonio enjoyed the comforts of the big automobile on warm summer evenings!

Because civilians wished to entertain the young pilots, Mac, a handsome captain, received many invitations to dinners and parties in town. He recalled one prominent San Antonio lumberman who constantly pressed him to go hunting at his duck club in Corpus Christi, guaranteeing Mac that he would get his limit. Mac knew absolutely nothing about hunting, but he eventually accepted the invitation. "They gave me a blind and a gun and the ducks flew out, and I didn't know what to do — or which ducks to shoot!"

Student instructors flew the JN4-D Jenny biplane. After a day's formal flying instruction had ended at five o'clock, Mac and the other pilots often went up for "joy rides," simulating dogfights and practicing dives, rolls, or steep climbs. Mac cryptically recorded one near tragedy in his logbook: "Solo . . . ran through fence . . . May 3."

When a pilot checked out for a long flight and failed to return, the base organized a search. Every pilot volunteered to help, re-flying the lost aircraft's route until they could locate the wreckage. Then they brought back the body. The group was close-knit, and each loss was a real and personal one for those who remained.

As the officer in charge of the field, Mac's job was to organize and initiate standard procedures for base personnel to follow in all conceivable situations. One of his first actions was to write and publish a booklet entitled *Manual of Administration of an Air Service Flying School*. He also wrote a smaller publication of even greater significance, *The All Thru System of Flying Instruction as Taught at Brooks Field*, that became the first basic flight manual for the air base and, in all likelihood, the forerunner of the current-day *Private Pilot Manual*. Mac patterned his manual after the one used by the Royal Air Force School of Flying at Gosport, England.

The Gosport System was developed after two years of war that had cost the Royal Air Force an appalling number of pilots and aircraft at the front and in training schools. The need for a more adequate and complete system of training was evident, and the result, through the efforts of RAF Colonel R. Smith Barry, was the Gosport System. The essential features of this system were: 1) the use of the speaking tube so that the instructor could communicate at all times with the student; 2) the correction of mistakes in the air right when they are made, "which is the proper time to make corrections"; 3) the assignment of one instructor for each student who was responsible for the student's progress throughout the complete course; and 4) the rigorous final testing in all maneuvers covered in the course of training. In this way, incompetent instructors and/or students could be weeded out.

Mac's booklet for the U.S. Air Service was a step-by-step manual on how to fly a plane, and included such general cautions to the student pilots:

Be sure your mind is working at least one step ahead of your machine so you will always know where your ship will be after the next move. . . . Flying is a brainy game and boobs will not last long. . . . Always have a possible landing field in sight and keep within gliding distance of it.

Conscientious and thorough, Mac often worked late into the night going over field assignments, although he longed to join his fellow officers in the barrack's lounge as they played poker, told stories, and joked. Mac received numerous unexpected honors for his hard work, including being chosen as the official pilot for a tour of the area by Prince Axel of Denmark, just before the signing of the Armistice in 1918.

By the time Mac left Brooks Field in June 1919, he had logged 768 hours of flight time. His next assignment would be the most important and dangerous of his career.

. . . This new era was full of adventure and excitement for the coura-geous. One of the more talented young designers . . . at McCook was Donald Douglas, who later achieved fame and fortune with his Douglas World Cruisers and Douglas Observation Planes.

Chapter 3

Coast-to-Coast, Hour Two

Signs of Trouble

THE T-2 HAD BEEN ALOFT for a short time when Mac felt the controls waggle between his knees — a signal for him to grab the stick and fly from the rear cockpit.

"Now why the hell did he do that?" Mac wondered. "He just started his shift, and he knows damned well how difficult it is to fly back here."

Assuming that Kelly wanted to check his maps, scratch, or change his position, Mac took the stick, anticipating he would return the control to the front cockpit within a few minutes.

Unknown to Mac, the ignition voltage regulator had been registering "discharge," indicating that the aircraft was flying entirely on battery power. Kelly painstakingly attempted to remove the delicate mechanism and adjust the breaker points within it so that it registered correctly. Sweat dripped from his brow as he worked; if he failed to fix the problem, their flight was over.

Mac was still flying the plane, growing increasingly irritated when, a half-hour after he had taken the controls, the stick waggled again. He shook his head in disbelief. But, a few minutes later he received a note from the front of the plane explaining Kelly's emergency repair efforts. Slightly embarrassed, he silently apologized to his partner for questioning his judgment.

The Fokker T-2 monoplane continued on its 80-mile-per-hour journey.

Flying Blind —
Pioneering Experiments and Developments at McCook Field

Walking through the gates at McCook Field in Dayton to his new assignment, in June 1919, Mac stopped to read the warning painted above the hangar door: "THIS FIELD IS SMALL, USE IT ALL."

Mac found Ralph DePalma, a former automobile racer and the base's officer in charge of flying, in a second-floor, glass-walled office that overlooked the field. He walked up to the desk and saluted smartly. "Lieutenant Macready reporting, Sir."

"Good morning, Macready, " DePalma said, as he got up and thrust out his hand in greeting. "You're just in time this morning. We're flight testing a new plane. Come on out with me, and we'll watch the action. Then we'll see about your duties and assignment."

As they walked out of the hangar, the piercing wail of a siren split the air. "My God, someone's crashed already," Mac thought, assuming the siren belonged to an ambulance. Men in military uniforms and secretaries in long, tight skirts rushed from every exit onto the flying apron. DePalma turned casually to the new pilot and reassured him that the siren signaled the start of a test flight — not the end.

The aircraft, being tested for the first time, sat on the flight line while receiving a final check by the mechanics. Captain Jones, the test pilot, stood by the plane, making sure the mechanics overlooked nothing. When ready, he climbed into the cockpit, waved at the assembled spectators, and gave the signal to the mechanics to turn the propeller. The motor caught, the prop turners ducked out of the way, and, after a short warm-up, the pilot gave the thumbs-up signal to pull the chocks from under the wheels.

Jones taxied down the field to the end of the runway where he maneuvered the aircraft around in a turn. Giving it full throttle, he roared across the runway, slowly gaining altitude as the wheels left the ground. He pulled the stick back and climbed to about 700 feet.

The test seemed to be going well until, after appearing to pause, or stall, with its nose up, the plane fell off to the right in a steep spiraling dive. The spectators' cheers of encouragement choked in their throats as the aircraft dropped to the earth in front of them and immediately burst into flames. Captain Jones had no chance to get out; he was burned beyond recognition.

DePalma turned to Mac. "Well, Macready, as you can see, we need replacements; let's get back and sign you on as a test pilot."

A short time after Captain Jones's accident, a new administration at the airfield improved pre-flight testing procedures. Prior to an actual test flight, all aircraft were taxied, turned, tested for ground-loop tendencies, and flown at different speeds just a few feet above the ground. Nevertheless, testing new airplanes remained a dangerous occupation.

McCook Field, named for "The Fighting McCooks" of Civil War fame, bordered the Miami River about two miles north of the Dayton business district. Established by the U.S. Army, in 1917, to compensate for its lack of progress with combat aircraft, McCook was where new airplanes were developed and tested. Although the Army had acquired its first plane from the Wright Brothers in 1909, little had changed in the way of design since then.

After World War I ended, the Army imported to McCook some of the foreign aircraft that had seen service during the war: Nieuports, Spads, Sopwith Camels, Capronis, Farmans, and Fokkers. Some had been taken as the spoils of war, others had been purchased.

But not all of the aircraft at McCook came from the war. As "aviation fever" spread across America in the early 1920s, inventors and hobbyists brought their airplanes to McCook for development and testing. Sometimes they built their inventions in a barn or garage at home before going to Dayton.

The test pilots and engineers at McCook weeded out the impossible aircraft ideas and identified the "possibilities" for further study. The engineering division checked out a plane's "flyability" on paper before the pilots subjected it to rigorous flight tests. Sperry-Messenger brought its new plane to McCook for testing, as did the Thomas Morse Chain Works, which brought its MB-3.

This new era was full of adventure and excitement for the courageous. One of the more talented young designers Mac met at McCook was Donald Douglas, who later achieved fame and fortune with his Douglas World Cruisers and Douglas Observation Planes.

Although the McCook engineering shops were equipped to construct an aircraft from nose to tail, the men needed the raw materials with which to build an airplane, and some of the most essential of these were scarce. Spruce wood, for example, the foundation of any airplane, was unobtainable in the quality and quantity needed. And so the engineers sent the "spruce production division" into the forests of the American Northwest to cut, saw, and season raw lumber.

Linen, which was used as a covering for the wings and fuselage, was also unavailable, both during and right after the war. And so textile experts at McCook invented a cotton fabric equal — and in some ways superior — to linen, and at half the cost. Engineers spent endless hours perfecting the propeller, switching its construction from balsa wood to duralumin, and redesigned radiators to remain cool at high altitudes. And they found the ideal sod for rain-soaked runways.

After his arrival at McCook Field, Mac found a room in a nearby house and settled into the daily life of a test pilot. One of his first assignments was to fly photographs of the Willard-Dempsey fight from Toledo, Ohio, to New York in time for publication in the newspapers the next morning. Jack Dempsey, the 187-pound, 24-year-old challenger, gave Jess Willard,

the 245-pound, 35-year-old defending heavyweight champion, a terrible
beating. The photos were "worth a thousand words."

On the night of July 4, 1919, Mac and his mechanic, Oscar Tripett,
waited in a field outside the Toledo arena for the fight to end. As the photographer rushed out with his pictures, Tripett cranked up the propeller.
Mac took the envelope and dropped it into his lap. The crowd was still
leaving the arena as the plane took off and climbed directly overhead en
route to New York. Suddenly, 200 feet over the arena, the engine quit.
Making a split-second decision, Mac swung the DeHavilland USD9AB
around as sharply as he could and brought it down over a National Guard
encampment, where it crashed in the open spaces among the tents. The
large plane, which was totally wrecked by the crash, flipped up and over
on its back. Fortunately, the accident injured no bystanders — just the
pilot and his mechanic. The prized photographs went to New York by
train.

Mac's fellow test pilots — Lieutenants Johnson, Hoy Barksdale,
Hutchinson, Moffett, Lockwood, Tourtellot, and Amis — were a cheerful,
optimistic group, all working in one of the world's most hazardous indus-
tries. To avoid worrying over the probability of crashing to their death —
they had witnessed too many tragedies to ignore it entirely — the fliers
developed a wonderfully macabre sense of humor.

Louie Meister was the biggest prankster of them all. One day his fellow
pilots, who often found themselves on the receiving end of his practical
jokes, decided to play a joke on him. All the pilots gathered for a "special
meeting" in the auditorium. As they filed in, one of them made sure Meister sat in a predesignated chair in the center of the room that had been
wired with electricity so that when someone pushed a button at the speaker's table, a stiff jolt passed through the chair's occupant.

The chairman walked up to the podium and began speaking in a voice
filled with emotion. "We are gathered together here this afternoon for a
very special reason," he intoned. "One of our most trusted and loyal
employees has a daughter who needs a very expensive operation to save
her life. The family has limited financial means, but they are good, hard-
working people, and we want to help them out. Now what do you say,
fellows? Shall we take up a collection to help this family?"

A resounding "yes!" filled the auditorium.

"All right then," said the chairman. "We'll start right now. Who wants to be the first to stand up and volunteer a donation. Let's start it off with, say twenty-five dollars." Unnoticed by his audience, he pressed the button.

Louie Meister was not known for his generosity. His fellow pilots called him "the biggest tightwad on the post." But when that electrical jolt went through him, he involuntarily leaped to his feet, becoming an instant big-spender — a philanthropist and a contributor.

"There's our first volunteer," shouted the chairman, gleefully. "Good for you, Louie! Twenty-five dollars from Louie Meister. Men, what do you think of that?"

The crowd gave a big shout of approval. Meister's boisterous protests were drowned by the cheers of the surrounding pilots as they jumped to their feet and pounded him on the back, congratulating him on his "generous donation."

Among the experiments at McCook were numerous flops, including the Gerhardt Cycle Plane. This contraption evolved from an argument between two factions of research engineers; one insisted that a bicycle-powered plane could never get off the ground, and the other felt that it could build one that would.

Fred Gerhardt, a flight research engineer, and E. L. Pratt, a flight test observer, went to work on the idea. Pratt completed the first layout in February 1923. The finished aircraft had six stacked wings, each with a 40-foot span, that rose 18 feet above the fuselage. The plane was, in a word, ugly.

The work continued secretly. Then, in October, Gerhardt and Pratt wheeled out their creation. Mac arrived to direct the show, and photographers came to take pictures. Gerhardt climbed into position on the seat, his feet on the pedals. The towing tug moved forward, and Gerhardt began frantically pumping the pedals. But immediately after the plane cleared the ground, its rigidity gave way, and the fuselage slowly and gently folded in two, its wings collapsing gracefully backward. The Gerhardt Cycle Plane's demise complete, it was returned in disgrace to its hayloft.

When word of the clandestine experiment leaked out, an official note appeared on the engineering bulletin board: "There will be no more un-authorized flights on this field!"

◌℘◌

But not every experiment ended in disaster. The test pilots and engineers at McCook could proudly point to many successes, even some that were unexpected. One earlier success began with a telephone call on August 31, 1921, from the commanding officer, Colonel Thurman H. Bane.

"Get up to my office right away, Macready. I've got some men here who want you as a pilot for a special test we've got going today."

When Mac arrived moments later, he saw several civilians seated around the room.

"These men are from the Department of Agriculture," Bane explained, proceeding to introduce each one. "They want us to help them with some controlled crop-dusting experiments. You'll take the bug dust up in the plane. Dormoy, the engineer, will go with you, in back, to operate the hoppers he's been working on. These men will tell you where and when they want the stuff dropped."

Mac was skeptical. Although some dusting experiments had been conducted a couple of years earlier, the results had been unsuccessful, and the project was dropped. Crops were typically sprayed from the ground, but lugging several thousand feet of hose over sometimes difficult terrain made the job expensive.

The Army Air Service had become involved with the dusting project after H. A. Gossard, chief of the Ohio Department of Entomology, had asked McCook Field for help. The idea began with C. R. Neille, of the Cleveland Parks Department, who had been spraying tall trees located in rugged terrain near the city in the summer of 1921, when he thought of using a plane or dirigible for distributing the chemicals. He discussed the idea with H. A. Gossard, who then turned to the Air Service.

Colonel Bane asked engineer Etienne Dormoy to make an apparatus for releasing the "bug powder" from an airplane. Dormoy designed two sifters, on the principle of an ordinary flour sifter, arranged with sprockets and chain drive, so that they could be operated from inside the plane. He fastened these sifters, with their flat hoppers, to the sides of the fuselage.

Although the Ohio Department of Entomology had originally planned to eradicate an infestation of canker worms, another bug caught the scientists' attention. Gossard explained the situation to Mac:

> A phenomenal outbreak of Catalpa Sphinx Moth has broken out on the farm of Mr. H. B. Carver at Casstown, near Troy, Ohio, not more than thirty miles north of here. There are about six acres of trees, literally alive with the caterpillars which have already denuded several valuable groves at different points. There must have been three hatches of these moths, because three new crops of foliage have been destroyed during the past season alone.

Mac readied his plane by having it rolled out of the hangar and fueled. A 32-gallon hopper tank filled with arsenate of lead was installed on the right side of the fuselage with the tank's sliding door positioned to allow smooth flow of the powder. At 3:00 p.m., Mac climbed into the front cockpit, still skeptical of the experiment; with Dormoy in the rear, they took off in the direction of Casstown.

Gossard and his Entomology Department men had gone on ahead by car and would meet them there.

Flying through a clear blue sky and a slight breeze, Mac let the plane descend gradually to 20 feet above the ground, skimming the tree tops. Then, leveling out and maintaining an airspeed of 80 mph, he flew along the windward side of the grove. In the back, Dormoy ground out his powdery poison by lifting the hopper door about seven inches. The powder, caught in the vacuum caused by the plane's slipstream, spread out over the grove where it settled on the trees. Dormoy turned a rotary fan, which prevented compacting or clogging and maintained an even outflow. Six times Mac flew back-and-forth over the grove, and six times Dormoy let the powder fly. They completed each pass in nine seconds and the whole process in less than a minute.

Within moments of the dusting, dead caterpillars covered the ground.

Mac landed in a adjoining field and found the Entomology men in the grove inspecting the dusting. When they saw him and Dormoy, they ran towards the airmen, shouting and waving their arms.

Concerned, Mac turned to Dormoy and wondered what could be the problem.

"I don't know," Dormoy said. "Maybe we killed the trees instead of the bugs!"

But as Gossard and his men rushed closer, Mac and Dormoy discovered what they were trying to tell them: "A great test. Not a tree branch that didn't have dust on it! Think what this means to the farmers! Remarkable coverage!" The men were ecstatic over the successful and important results.

Mac and Dormoy flew back to McCook, entirely unaware that by dropping a load of pesticide over the Catalpa grove they had made entomological history, having demonstrated the first successful aerial crop-dusting. For Mac, this was another "first" that he took in stride.

Mac eventually became McCook's chief test pilot as well as its officer in charge of flying. In addition to his duties testing experimental aircraft, his job required him to host distinguished guests. One morning, he received word that Colonel Bane wanted to see him right away. He walked briskly across the field and, upon entering the commanding officer's office, threw a snappy salute before his desk.

"Yes, Sir! You wanted to see me?"

"Macready," Bane barked. "That wild man Mitchell's coming out here again to look at our planes. What have you got for him to see?"

"Well, we've got the Le Pére LUSAC-11 I've been doing the high altitude flights with and a Thomas Morse MB-3 biplane that looks promising, and some others I'll check on . . . ," Mac was thinking out loud.

"Well, get what you have out on the line. He'll be here tomorrow morning, early," Bane said.

Brigadier General William E. "Billy" Mitchell, the assistant chief of the Air Service, was famous for his limitless drive and his monumental impatience.

When he arrived, the planes were lined up facing the center of a half circle. The test pilots stood beside their planes, and waited to answer his rapid-fire questions. Mitchell came out to the edge of the field where Mac joined his tour. The General asked about each aircraft, barely waiting for the answer before rushing on to the next question.

"What's this one, Bane?" he asked the Colonel. Bane gave him a technical description of the plane, but Mitchell didn't like the answer. So he turned to Mac.

"How does it maneuver in flight? What's its airspeed? How high and how fast does it climb? What's the ceiling?"

Mac responded as quickly as the questions came. "This one has a tendency to ground loop; that one over there skids in the turns; the one on the end is sluggish and doesn't respond well to the controls."

When they came to the Le Pére LUSAC-ll biplane, Mac said proudly, "This is the high-altitude plane we've installed with the supercharger." He had been testing this plane himself.

The Le Pére, built by Packard in 1918, was the first Army aircraft equipped with a turbo-supercharged 400-hp engine, the Liberty-12 model, and had a top speed of 133 mph and a ceiling of 34,000 feet.

Mitchell appeared interested, so Mac detailed the problems he had encountered and what he was doing to correct them.

After completing his inspection, Mitchell turned to Mac and ordered him to "get these planes ready to fly and we'll try them out." He handed Mac a list of the aircraft that interested him, and that afternoon he went up in each of them, sometimes handling the controls himself, more often riding as a passenger while the test pilot put the plane through its paces.

Billy Mitchell was an aggressive, sometimes abrupt man, but, he was a dedicated champion of a strong and separate air force. Although not the most skilled pilot in the world, he had what, at the time, was equally important — guts. But when he insisted on taking up the Le Pére biplane, Mac tried to dissuade him.

"If you haven't flown this type of ship before, Sir, you should watch out when you land. It has a heavy metal gear which makes it real tricky to bring down. Want me to check you out first?" Mac asked, as concerned about the aircraft as he was about Mitchell.

"Nope, I'll take it up myself," the General replied.

Mitchell did, and his landing made Mac's heart race in fear. The Le Pére bounced and ground looped dangerously before rolling to a stop. When the flight was over, Mac breathed a sigh of relief.

To prepare for a high-altitude flight in his supercharged Le Pére, Mac had slipped on several pairs of wool socks and high-topped, fleece-lined, elk-hide moccasins with moose-hide soles for protection against the minus 80 degree F temperatures. His jacket had several built-in pockets to keep items handy — an extra pair of goggles and a handkerchief to wipe them if they iced up. The biplane had an open cockpit, so even with all this protective covering he would be unbearably cold.

Of course, being cold was better than being electrocuted. Mac remembered a French flying suit fitted with wires for electric heating that a McCook test pilot had dubbed "an electrocuting straight-jacket." His scorched underwear had supported his claim.

Mac picked up the leather, fur-lined head mask and pulled it firmly over his head, leaving only his eyes, nose, and mouth exposed for the oxygen mask and goggles. Glancing in the mirror, he thought how frightening he would look to anyone who didn't know what he was, for he looked more like a creature from outer space than a man.

Mac walked into the hangar to watch the technicians install the barographs in the rear cockpit of the Le Pére. These instruments recorded atmospheric pressure, supercharger pressure, and altitude on smoked paper. When the installation was finished, Mac climbed into the Le Pére and gave the signal for the mechanics to turn the propeller. The Liberty engine caught, the prop whirred, and the biplane taxied slowly out for takeoff, while Mac checked his instrument readings as he pulled his goggles over his face mask. Sliding on his thick, fur-lined gloves, he pushed the throttle lever forward, waved his hand to the group assembled to watch the takeoff, and rolled down the runway. He remembered the day, a month earlier, when he had helped pull the limp figure of Rudolph "Shorty" Schroeder, unconscious and sightless, from this very plane.

During Schroeder's flight in the Le Pére, his automatic oxygen supply had failed, and he had switched to his emergency supply. But after climbing to over 25,000 feet, the oxygen in his emergency tank gave out, too. Lifting his goggles momentarily as he leaned over to adjust the tanks, he lost consciousness. His plane plunged downward out of control for over five miles. He was lucky, though, because at 2,000 feet he came to and, although nearly blind and in great pain, he managed to pull the nose up out of the dive and into level flight. Recognizing the shape of the McCook Field Hospital directly below him, Schroeder decided to land the plane from memory. When the men on the field reached him, he was unable to move. His eyelids were swollen shut, his eyeballs frozen.

Immediately following this incident, Mac took over the high-altitude experimental work.

As Mac took off into the leaden skies for his own high-altitude test, he took the Le Pére in a slow, steady climb. As he reached 20,000 feet, with plenty of power remaining, the outside temperature began a steep plunge. The aircraft's thermometers could record temperatures only to 45 degrees F below zero; the needle on his plane had run completely off the drum.

The big 400-hp Liberty-12 engine, which was designed to burn fuel mixed with air at a sea-level pressure of 14.7 pounds per square inch, began to slow, and Mac knew he would have to cut in the supercharger. Without it, the engine would drop to 87 hp, which was hardly enough to keep the plane level. The supercharger cut in on command, giving the biplane a sudden increase in power and airspeed. Mac wrapped one hand — which was icy even inside its glove — around the stick while he used the other to turn on the oxygen. He knew he needed oxygen right away when he had inverted a written temperature reading — a sign of hypoxia. He put the tube in his mouth, turned the knob, and took in deep breaths of pure oxygen.

The cold began to penetrate his layered clothing as the altimeter passed 25,000 feet. Then he heard a sudden loud whir; he felt a rush of air, a sharp jar, a violent wrench, and a jerk. The propeller had spun itself right off its hub and had crashed through the struts between the biplane's wings. With nothing to hold them steady, the wings wobbled dangerously as the wind whipped through them. The airspeed indicator showed that the plane had slowed alarmingly, while the rpm indicator showed a tremendous speedup. Mac turned off the supercharger before he lost the engine completely.

"Damn. This is a helluva fix," he thought, as he gently pushed the stick forward, leaning the biplane into a slow descent. "Better go slow, pressure will start building up too fast on my body," he told himself, steering in wide circles to stay above McCook Field. He spiraled slowly downward, intent on maintaining his airspeed and altitude until he could find the field below and maneuver the aircraft over it.

His landing was uneventful. But when he arrived in the pilot's lounge, it erupted with loud boisterous laughter. "Lost your prop, did you, Mac? We'll have a treasure hunt to see who finds it first!" Off they ran, scurrying across the fields in search of Mac's lost propeller.

Later, Mac learned that using a standard Liberty engine propeller at high altitudes was a grievous mistake, the thin air above 20,000 feet caused it to revolve too fast. He knew that the propeller branch was experimenting with variable-pitch props, so he waited for one of the new propellers to be installed on the Le Pére before trying another high-altitude flight.

After numerous tests with variable-pitch props, the McCook engineers installed an oversized propeller on the Le Pére. This was a great idea, but the engineers had forgotten one small detail: when you pushed forward the throttle of a tail-dragger plane, the tail lifted for taxiing, the nose descended, and the prop dug right into the ground.

On a subsequent flight, Mac took the Le Pére to 30,400 feet before the supercharger flew apart, its bolts and bearings tearing loose, the buckles flying out of the turbine wheel, and metal parts shooting off in all directions, forcing a quick retreat to the field.

Mac's three separate high-altitude test flights in the Le Pére, during July and August 1921, ended abruptly between 26,000 and 27,000 feet, because the supercharger ignited early. Dense black smoke poured from the engine, forcing him to bring the plane down. The supercharger went in for repairs and Mac went on to other tests.

By September, the supercharger had been repaired and reinstalled, so Mac resumed his daily high-altitude tests. However, the supercharger continued to give him trouble, but within a few weeks, it operated with relative dependability. After consulting with his superiors, he decided to make an attempt at the world-altitude record, which, to the Air Service's dismay, was held by the French.

The *Fédération Aéronautique Internationale* (FAI) had been established as the official body for air speed and high-altitude records, in Paris in 1905. As U.S. representative, Orville Wright came to McCook to observe and confirm the results of Mac's high-altitude flight. He was meticulous in his technical requirements because he knew that the slightest irregularity in any recording instrument would allow the FAI to disclaim the flight's validity.

On the morning of September 18, 1921, Mac climbed into the modified Le Pére, flipped the ignition switch, and signaled for the prop to be turned, then pulled his goggles down over his eyes and slipped on his fur-lined gloves. The engine caught, and the mechanic beat a hasty retreat.

Because the biplane had no brakes, turning the knife-sharp blades put mechanics in danger. So they quickly grew accustomed to dodging revolving blades — and few ever died in the process. (General Billy Mitchell, who preferred to start a plane himself, would tie one end of a rope to the tail of his craft and the other end around a tree before spinning the prop, having stationed some hardy soul nearby to cut the rope, while he returned to the cockpit.)

Mac checked his instruments. Although the exterior strut thermometer read a comfortable 70 degrees F, he knew it would drop drastically when he gained sufficient altitude. Locating the supercharger knob on the lower-left side of the cockpit near the engine spark and throttle controls, he moved it back and forth to see that it operated freely. Altogether, he had 22 instruments to watch or operate. Orville Wright's instruments had replaced Roy Langham, Mac's observer, in the rear cockpit.

Mac missed Langham; they had been a real team. As he prepared to head up into the sky alone, he remembered one flight on which he had almost lost Langham. Against Mac's better judgment, they had gone up one morning when the sky was completely overcast. Once above the clouds, they flew a level course with the throttle wide open. As their test neared completion, an engine fire ignited, shooting out flames on both sides. Dense smoke poured out from under the cowling into the cockpits, enveloping them in a blinding, choking, dark cloud. Mac pushed the stick full forward and plunged down through the clouds in an effort to extinguish the flames. Although his efforts worked, the engine continued to smoke.

By this time, Mac had lost his bearings. He couldn't find Dayton or any familiar landmarks for navigation. So he turned around in the cockpit, always an awkward maneuver in the heavy flight suit, and tried to indicate by hand signals — in this case, pointing decisively toward the ground — that he was lost. Then he turned back to focus his attention on flying the aircraft. After receiving no return signal from Langham, he turned around again, just in time to see his observer preparing to jump out. He had misinterpreted the hand signal as a gesture to abandon ship, thinking they were going to crash. Mac grabbed Langham just before he jumped and pulled him back into the cockpit. Because parachutes were still in the experimental stage, Mac had probably saved Langham's life.

Although their flight came close to disaster, the two airmen had learned an important lesson: fuel catches on fire when flying at full throttle at high altitudes.

కుర్

Wright signaled Mac to take off that September morning. The mechanics pulled the chocks from under the wheels, and the Le Pére taxied down the runway, gradually gaining enough speed for the liftoff as Mac eased the stick back.

Keeping the nose pointed upward in a steady climb, Mac could feel the drop in temperature through his heavy suit. At 20,000 feet, he circled slowly to let his body adjust to the pressure change and turned on his oxygen tube. The air grew even colder as the altimeter moved past the 30,000 foot mark. His hands stiffened, which made manipulating the control wires increasingly difficult. The wires had contracted and tightened when the lubricating oil on the pulleys, over which they operated, froze.

Despite the toll on his bodily comfort, the severe cold left the supercharger unfazed. If it continued to perform perfectly, Mac might just make that record flight Orville was anticipating and bring the altitude record back to the United States. At 35,000 feet, the plane began to respond sluggishly, yet Mac maintained pressure on the stick and thrust upward past the 38,000-foot mark.

His goggles began to ice up despite the antifreeze, which supposedly worked to minus 60 degrees F. As the icing reduced his visibility, Mac decided to risk taking off his goggles to clean them. But within the few seconds his eyes remained unprotected from the blast of the propeller, tears formed and turned to icicles. The pain was so intense, he cried out to an empty sky.

At that point his mind began to grow fuzzy; the instrument panel was swimming in front of him. Glancing at the airspeed indicator, Mac noted with surprise that it read 65 mph. Then he realized he was actually looking at the tachometer, which recorded the 1650 rpms. The propeller blurred out of focus, then disappeared altogether. "I'm losing it," he told himself. "I'm losing consciousness!"

Mac recognized the signs of oxygen starvation, the creeping euphoric feeling that swept over the mind and body. As the altimeter neared 40,000 feet, he sat perfectly still, knowing that the least movement or expenditure of energy would make him irrational. He needed more oxygen.

Suspecting that the main flask had become clogged, he peeled the adhesive plaster off the side of his mask, cracked open the emergency flask, turned the nozzle, and stuck it into his mouth. He felt immediate relief. But when he started spitting ice chunks from his mouth, he realized what the problem had been. Ice had clogged the main tube, almost causing a tragedy.

The altimeter inched toward 41,000 feet. Without the supercharger, the Le Pére had only a ceiling of 15,000 feet. The supercharger simulated sea-level atmospheric conditions for the engine at high altitudes by forcing an increased amount of the less dense air into the engine's carburetor. It enabled the aircraft to maintain engine power in the rarefied atmosphere above 25,000 feet.

The biplane strained to climb a few more feet, but reached its absolute ceiling at 41,200. It wallowed around in the light air, suspended in space, rising sluggishly 20 or 30 feet, then dropping back down. Mac took a look around for the first time. The sky was a dazzling white, almost blinding in its intensity. He noticed a few small feathery clouds floating just above him. He was higher at that moment than any man had ever been before. And he was humbled by the realization, as put forth by another aviator some years later, that he had "trod the untrespassed sanctity of space, reached out his hand, and touched the face of God."

Mac's moment of realization and wonder came to a sudden end as he felt the paralyzing cold pierce his heavy suit. "Can't take much more of this," he thought. After taking one last look at the altimeter's reading of 41,200 feet, he pushed the stick gently forward and descended in ever-widening spirals, easing the throttle back as the aircraft gained speed. He had left the supercharger control knob unbothered, but his slight let-up on the throttle caused the engine to quit. Without the engine, his cockpit radiation system, which provided him with some warmth, ceased to generate heat. His goggles froze again. The biplane started falling out of control; at 30,000 feet, pressure began to build up in his eardrums. Mac pushed the throttle forward full bore in an attempt to start the engine; it sputtered on, then off. "Come on baby, you can do it," he muttered under his breath.

Finally it caught, allowing Mac to level off before continuing his slow circular descent, pausing every 5,000 feet to let his body adjust. By that time, the pressure in his ears had become agonizing throbs.

❧

Attempting to overcome problems with pressure, the Army Air Corps had developed a barrel-shaped steel pressure cabin. Two six-inch glass windows offered the pilot limited visibility. Yet when Mac gave the contraption a test run, the valve that relieved cabin pressure failed to work as quickly as the outside air pressure had increased. Mac couldn't open the steel door to equalize the two pressures, so he slowly circled toward the ground until he could make a half-blind landing.

The general opinion after this flight was that the lack of sufficient air pressure on Mac's body was less dangerous to him than being cooped up in a metal coffin, and the pressure cabin contraption was sent to the McCook Museum.

❧

When Mac finally landed at McCook Field that day, he felt as if he had just come from a world beyond anything he had ever known — certainly a world no one else had ever seen. He was awestruck by the enormity of the experience.

Orville Wright and the officials from the FAI hurried over when the plane came to a stop.

"Did you make it?" Wright asked, excitedly.

"How high did you go?" someone else asked.

"What was it like?" added Wright. The questions spilled out one after the other.

"Let's just wait and see what the instruments say," Mac answered, grinning. "The altimeter indicated 41,200 feet at the ceiling."

But when the engineering department finished calibrating the instruments for corrected readings, it brought the figure down to 40,800 feet. The Bureau of Standards's computation set the figure at 39,700, and later, under still another method of figuring, reduced it to 37,800 feet. Finally, the FAI brought the figure down to 34,563 feet.

But even at the lower figure, Mac had a world record.

Orville Wright came into Mac's office later to give him the good news.

The base celebrated. On September 18, 1921, through the efforts of Lieutenant John A. Macready, the United States of America held the new world-altitude record.

The official figures were based on the commonly held assumption of the time that the temperature is constant at any altitude, no matter how high the plane climbs. Mac contended, however, and it was later corroborated, that the temperature constantly changes as the plane ascends into the atmosphere. Therefore, he believed that the official altitude figures should have been based on that assumption, which would put his altitude record flight close to the original figures. Although the higher figures were later proved accurate, he was not given credit for them.

. . . In a desperate effort to cool down the engine and continue the flight, the pilots began pouring into it every liquid they could find — the remains of the consommé, the coffee, and their drinking water. . . . Just when it began to look as if they could actually make it, engine trouble had thwarted their flight.

Chapter 4

Coast-to-Coast, Hour Seven

Spotted Over Dayton

O N THE MORNING OF APRIL 15, 1923, when Mac and Oakley Kelly had left McCook Field for New York, Lieutenants Clarence Crumrine and T. C. McMahon promised to meet and escort the T-2 when it would pass over McCook, enroute to its destination at San Diego. "When we see you coming, we'll fly out to cheer you up a bit. And when you see us waving, you'll know it's me and McMahon," Crumrine told Mac.

After learning of the T-2's successful takeoff on May 2nd, Crumrine and McMahon followed all the radio reports and the progress of the flight. They kept a plane tuned and ready for their aerial greeting. And when the two lieutenants heard that the T-2 had been sighted over a small town at the Pennsylvania-Ohio border, McMahon suggested that they climb to the top of the water tower to watch for the approaching plane. As they turned their eyes toward the eastern horizon, every bird took the shape of an airplane, sending the men scurrying to their cockpits. But when the sun began to cast long shadows across the field, the two men began to despair.

Then, McMahon shouted from his perch, "I think I see them. Hand me the telescope, quick." The telescope was the 99-cent variety. "Here they come! You take a look," he said, handing the instrument to Crumrine.

"I see the plane. It's headed straight for us!" Crumrine shouted, just as a slightly blind beetle flew into the telescope lens.

A moment later, the radio operator called from the hangar doorway to say that T-2 had then passed over Richmond, Indiana. Crumrine and McMahon had watched in vain.

That evening, the Air Service pilots held an elaborate ceremony to award the two chagrined lieutenants the "Alibi Trophy."

The T-2 had reached Dayton ahead of schedule. Mac and Kelly had planned to circle McCook and waggle their wings, but "we had considerable flying ahead of us and were anxious to be on our way," Mac explained later.

Lieutenants Harris, Ackerman, and Brookley had also been waiting by their aircraft for the T-2 to pass over the field. When it flew steadily across the sky, they jumped in their planes and gave chase, overtaking Mac and Kelly at Richmond. They escorted the T-2 all the way to Indianapolis before returning to McCook.

When Lieutenant Harris pulled up alongside the T-2 and waved, Mac, who had been absorbed in his duties in the front cockpit, smiled and waved back. But Kelly, who was always a showman, opened the cabin door and waved his bedding exuberantly from the side of the plane.

Initial Attempts at Non-Stop Transcontinental Flight

The year before the record-breaking flight, in 1922, on one of his rare visits to the McCook Field test-pilots' lounge, Colonel Bane had noticed a large map of the United States posted prominently on the wall. A dark line ran across the map from San Diego east through New Mexico, then up across Oklahoma, Kansas, and the Midwestern states, ending at Long Island, New York. "What's this?" he asked, pointing to the map.

Oakley Kelly seized the opportunity to pitch an idea to Bane. That map indicated a proposed route he and Mac wanted to follow on what would be the first non-stop, 2,500-mile flight across the continent. Without pausing, he described their plans, which had been made during the winter of 1921 and 1922, and the data already calculated for the flight. He told Bane that the Air Service's recently purchased $30,000 Fokker IV was the most suitable plane for a flight of this kind. Mac told Bane about the static tests the pilots had run on the wing and about the ceiling determinations they had used to ascertain the ability of the aircraft to clear the high points along their proposed route.

Bane liked their idea, and later, when the chief of the Air Service, Major General Mason M. Patrick, arrived at McCook Field on an inspection trip, in August 1922, Bane presented the plan to him. General Patrick approved the flight, and Mac and Kelly immediately began to prepare.

The Dutch-built Fokker IV was originally designed to carry eight to ten passengers in the cabin and a pilot up front in a single-place, open-air cockpit, along the left side of the engine. The thick-winged monoplane normally could carry 180 gallons of petrol, enough for about six hours of flight. But because Mac's and Kelly's intended flight would last up to 30 hours, the aircraft would need to hold more fuel. Accordingly, they installed an extra 410-gallon fuel tank between the spars at the center section of the wing, along with a 40-gallon oil tank. They added a ten-gallon reserve water tank, a booster radiator, an oil radiator, and a second set of controls — a control wheel and rudder pedals — was welded in the cabin near a door close to the third window at the left side of the fuselage. There, the "rear" pilot sat, at the ready, to relieve the forward pilot when rest was needed, either by pre-arranged time changes or, in an urgent situation, when the pilot up front would shake the control wheel.

Other modifications to the Fokker IV included a set of Army 44-by-10-inch wheels, a new set of Goodyear tires, and a folding seat in the forward pilot's cockpit, in front of a small opening into the cabin so that the two pilots could exchange places when taking their turns at the front controls. A hammock-like bench seat behind the rear controls allowed the relief pilot to stretch out and sleep, if time and conditions permitted.

With all this extra weight, the wings and fuselage required reinforcement. The engineering department substituted laminated wood for linen as a wing-covering material, and celluloid for glass in the doors and windows. Tubular steel was used to construct the fuselage. A new type of siphon pump fed gas to the motor, eliminating the need for an extra motor to increase air pressure, and reducing the chance of a fire. All of the modifications were designed, built, and installed in less than six weeks.

The pilot in the Fokker IV's outside cockpit did most of the flying, because he had an unobstructed view. The single 400-hp Liberty-12 engine, located in the nose to overcome torque and to allow more room inside, carried a gross load of more than five tons. However, its location, just eight inches from the pilot, left him to suffer through noise, vibration, and icy winds.

The Fokker IV was renamed the T-2 after a rumor had spread among the press and the general public that, so soon after World War I, the Air Service was going to use a "German" plane for such an important flight. In truth, the Fokker had been built in the Netherlands. Nevertheless, to preclude any criticism, the Air Service dropped the name "Fokker" from the plane's official designation, with the "T" in T-2 indicating transport. Despite this concession, public and press sentiment ran so high against foreign-built aircraft that the T-2 remained under heavy security.

As the modifications progressed, so did the planning for the transcontinental route. Mac and Kelly would need to fly over the Sierra Nevada Mountains, so they calculated their necessary altitude and how the initial load of 10,695 pounds would affect the plane's ability to reach it. While Mac was busy completing further tests on the supercharger, Kelly and Ernest W. Dichman made a flying survey of the terrain west of El Paso, Texas, noting possible emergency landing fields and passes or canyons through the more than 1,000 miles of mountainous country across which the T-2 would have to fly. Because the flying survey indicated that the T-2 would have enough climbing power to clear the mountains out of San

Diego, and because the prevailing winds traveled from west to east, they decided to fly in that direction.

◈

On September 19, 1922, Mac and Kelly began ferrying the T-2 west via St. Louis, Missouri, Lawton, Oklahoma, and El Paso, Texas, finally landing at Rockwell Field (now North Island Naval Air Base) in San Diego, California.

They chose sunrise, Thursday, October 5, 1922, as their takeoff date for the coast-to-coast flight. Workmen leveled the Rockwell Field runway and the ground at each end, removing grass, rocks, and bushes from the one-and-a-half mile strip. On Monday, October 2, Mac and Kelly took the big plane up for final tests and discovered that the runway was too soft; and thus, a longer, firmer strip of land was located, and the grass mowed. A red flag on the new runway marked the "point of no return" — the point after which, if the T-2 had failed to leave the ground, the pilot still had three-quarters of a mile to shut off the engine and abort the takeoff of the brake-less aircraft.

On Wednesday afternoon, October 4th, the mechanics rolled the T-2 from its hangar to give it a final check. Mac and Kelly carefully tested each control wire and wiped all the moisture from the fuselage to lessen skin friction and remove every ounce of extra weight; they filled the main and auxiliary tanks with Shell gasoline and the lubricant containers with Pennzoil motor oil.

As nighttime arrived, the huge plane glistened in the moonlight, its shape clearly outlined against the sky. Two elderly ladies, anxious to be on hand for the start of the flight, had driven to the field shortly before noon on Wednesday and parked at the very edge of the landing strip, nearest the T-2. Along with the other spectators, they made themselves comfortable for the long night of waiting, with blankets and a large hamper of edibles. The atmosphere felt like a carnival.

◈

Mac's parents, Mattie and Ben Macready, had traveled to San Diego Tuesday afternoon. That night Mac, Kelly, and the latter's "lady friend," Mary Watson, joined them for dinner at the U.S. Grant Hotel in downtown

San Diego. After dinner, although they had beds at the base hospital, the two pilots opted to spend their last night at the hotel.

Mac and Kelly arrived at the field at 5:25 a.m., Mac accompanied by his mother and father, Kelly by Mary Watson. Newspapermen representing all the major news services had gathered to cover the start of the flight.

Rockwell Field officials handed the pilots three-dozen letters to carry to New York, among them one from San Diego Mayor John L. Bacon to the Mayor of New York, "extending San Diego's greetings via the Langley and Wright Brothers Airways;" one from E. F. Parmafee, business manager of the *San Diego Union*, to O'Mara and Ormabee, *Union* and *Tribune* representatives in New York; and one from H. E. Morin of the *Union* editorial staff to William Bayard Swope of the *New York World*.

Mac self-consciously but affectionately kissed his mother good-bye in front of the cameras and shook hands with his father, while Kelly delighted the spectators by giving Mary Watson a long, passionate kiss. By previous agreement, they flipped a coin to determine who would pilot the plane on takeoff.

"Heads," Kelly yelled.

The coin came spiraling down to the dirt as everyone crowded forward to see the result.

"Heads it is!" shouted Kelly, who scrambled up into the nose of the ship, while Mac took his place inside the cabin.

Three mechanics — one gripping the propeller blades and the others holding onto his left arm to yank him to safety when the prop started — obeyed Kelly's instructions to turn the propeller. Two sharp yanks and the motor caught. After a few moments of warm-up, they pulled the chocks, and the heavy plane started to lumber slowly down the cleared strip, gathering momentum as it went. At a mere 300 feet from the starting point, the T-2 had barely reached 30 miles per hour.

The spectators — over 200 courageous souls — some who had slept there overnight, some who had risen long before dawn to witness the takeoff — watched in tense silence, mutely willing the aircraft to lift off. At the half-mile marker, the wheels cleared the ground for a second, then settled back down and continued rolling until, just short of the one-mile marker, the T-2 finally lifted off in an almost imperceptible rise.

Directly opposite Ballast Point Lighthouse, while still less than 74 feet above the waters of San Diego Bay, Kelly turned the T-2's nose toward the ocean.

Reaching the westerly end of North Island and hugging the shoreline, he turned the plane south and began a great circle around the island, gaining another 25 feet as they passed over the lighthouse a second time and managed to reach 200 feet as they swept back over the field.

Mac and Kelly were jubilant; they were on their way to the East Coast! Kelly raised himself slightly in the cockpit as he passed over the field and waved his left arm over his head once, then pointed toward the cloud-topped mountains to the northeast.

A tumultuous cheer went up from the spectators on the field, many of whom had tears in their eyes, as they watched the T-2 disappear toward the mountains.

To cross the Temecula Pass, west of San Diego, Mac and Kelly needed to climb to only 1,200 feet, but the cloudy weather forced them to go to more than 2,000 feet for safety. For one-and-a-half hours they attempted to coax the heavy plane above the cloud bank, flying in a loop from north to south. But the aircraft would climb no higher. In their fruitless search for the pass through the Laguna Mountains, they were using up precious fuel and the safety margin they needed to make a non-stop flight across the continent.

Mac later explained, "Kelly and I were a couple of young fellows who enjoyed living to the fullest extent, and we had absolutely no intention of committing suicide. To attempt to fly through those winding mountain passes at 100 mph, with a sluggish plane loaded to capacity, through fog so dense we couldn't see fifty feet ahead, would have been tantamount to putting the muzzle of a loaded pistol to the side of your head and pulling the trigger."

The two fliers passed notes back and forth, trying to make a decision. Eventually, they decided to turn back to San Diego, but instead of landing, they would attempt to break the world endurance record — another record held by the French. They had everything they needed: plenty of fuel, an excellent plane, and a pile of chicken sandwiches.

As the men flew back over San Diego, Mac wrote a note and addressed it to Captain Ervin, commanding officer of Rockwell Field:

Impossible to get through mountain passes with heavy load

on account of dense fog at ground and aloft. An hour and a half wasted in attempting to get through with no sign of clearing.

Cannot now reach the high altitudes south of Tucumcari, New Mexico, by nightfall. We are attempting to break the world's endurance record for airplanes and will make the transcontinental flight later. Please get in touch with representatives of the National Aeronautical Association and take the steps necessary to authenticate a world's airplane endurance record, should the attempt prove successful, and also wire this information to the commanding officer, McCook Field.

Folding up the note and placing it in a tin canister provided for just such communication, Mac attached a tiny weight tied with several small red, white, and blue streamers and dropped the note over the side of the plane. It landed on the roof of hangar number one, where the post adjutant retrieved it and passed it along.

Captain Ervin immediately began issuing orders

Get those big strips of linen out of the hangar and spread them out on the field so the boys will have something to aim at when they throw their messages down. And pull out the big searchlights so they'll be ready to turn on tonight to illuminate the field for them.

Then he contacted the NAA.

During his first shift over San Diego, Kelly throttled the motor down to 1,300 rpm from its peak of 1,490, keeping the plane in a shallow bank to the right at a constant altitude of 2,000 feet. Mac and Kelly had agreed to pilot for six-hour shifts, and toward the end of his first shift, as Kelly grew increasing fatigued, he sent a note fluttering down to the white linen strip below: "Just passed over the city and saw a sign that read, Kelly Tires. I'll say!"

Crawling forward for his stint at the controls, Mac inched through the narrow passageway between the cabin and the cockpit, while Kelly went back to relax. The procedure was reversed at six p.m. and again at midnight.

All through the long day, the T-2 circled above the city. During the moonlit night that followed, the steady thundering of the Liberty engine reminded slumbering San Diegans that the flight was continuing over their heads.

Officially, the attempt to break the endurance record would provide the pilots with reliable information on the T-2's fuel, oil, and water consumption under different load conditions and would determine if the aircraft could reach the 6,800-foot altitude needed to fly over the mountains near Santa Rosa, New Mexico. Unofficially, neither pilot wanted to land with a full load of fuel on board or so soon after having received such a tremendous publicity-laden farewell. Kelly, who had used the occasion to extract a particularly fond good-bye from Mary Watson, didn't want to disappoint her.

Friday dawned with a thick covering of fog hanging over the bay city, but by late morning it blew out to sea. As the T-2 continued its sweep, the pilots dropped messages to keep the men at Rockwell fully informed of their progress. At mid-morning, Kelly dropped another note:

> We have plenty of gasoline and oil but are out of tobacco. Will land just before dark as we have already spent a few hours in the air and do not want to land after dark.

Toward late afternoon, as the flight grew monotonous and the fuel ran low, Mac turned the aircraft in tighter circles over North Island. As anxious as a contestant in musical chairs, he anticipated running out of fuel by positioning the plane near a safe landing place. The engine's left exhaust manifold, three lugs on the long upward-extending exhaust stack, and the right upper side of the engine cowling had cracked. Both outside streamlining wheel covers had ripped from their retaining rings around the wheel hub, and the mounting screws in all the windows had cracked and loosened from the continuous vibration of the engine. The T-2 needed a rest.

At five o'clock on Friday afternoon, with only a few minutes worth of fuel in the tanks and a nighttime emergency landing looming, the two pilots agreed to set down while they could still safely do so. Mac rolled the T-2 up on one wing in a 45-degree bank and turned into the wind. The wheels touched down at 5:11 p.m. on October 6, 1922, as Mac, his face smeared with oil, his arms aching from his last six hours at the stick, brought the monoplane in for a perfect landing. He and Kelly had been in the air for 35 hours, 18 minutes, and 30 seconds, smashing the previous record of 26 hours and 19 minutes.

When Mac and Kelly climbed down, a swarm of well-wishers pressed forward, eager to shake their hands and offer congratulations. Mattie Macready forced her way through the waiting crowd and proudly flung her arms around her son.

Meanwhile, Kelly looked around for Mary, his own private welcoming committee. When he pulled away from the throng and greeted her with a passionate embrace, the cameramen were delighted.

⁓

Two days later, two French lieutenants named Bossoutrot and Droupin went up over LaBourget, France, in an attempt to wrest the endurance record from the two U.S. Air Service pilots. When they failed to break the American record, the French Aerial Federation announced that it considered the 34-hour, 16-minute flight of the French pilots a world mark, as the American flight had been conducted under conditions that would not be accepted by the *Fédération Aéronautique Internationale*. The American press accused the French Aero Club of poor sportsmanship — as did many U.S. Air Service pilots.

⁓

As Mac and Kelly waited for the weather to permit another cross-country flight, they grew increasingly anxious. Every time they stepped into the elevator at their hotel someone would ask when they intended to start the flight. For a week or so after the endurance flight, the two fliers answered the questions casually. But later on, as the sun shone brightly over San Diego, they found blaming their delay on the weather embarrassing. Mac and Kelly suspected that San Diegans were winking at each other, thinking that these two pilots knew a good thing when they saw one, that they preferred spending a nice warm winter in San Diego instead of returning to Ohio's cold and snow. San Diegans were unaware of the violent storms raging across the Midwest that would have made a non-stop cross-country flight suicidal.

One night, loud pounding on their door woke Mac and Kelly from a sound sleep. Kelly opened the door and found a deputy sheriff, who looked from one man to the other, and demanded, "Which one of you is Oakley Kelly?"

The deputy had a summons for Kelly from his wife, who was suing for divorce because she had seen a newspaper photograph of his embrace with Mary Watson.

～⁊⨾

On November 2, while Mac was giving a talk at the University Club's annual Duck Dinner, meteorologist Dean Blake arrived at the hotel.

"Well, Kelly, I think this may be it," Blake said, unrolling his weather charts and spreading them on the coffee table. "Here, take a look at this."

As the two men bent over the charts, Blake traced the proposed route with a pencil while pointing to the numbers and symbols indicating high- and low-pressure areas and the direction and velocity of winds.

"Indications are, as you can see, that there will be reasonably good weather with favorable winds along practically the entire route tomorrow. I'll call in to the office around nine tonight for the final report from the Weather Bureau chief in Washington. They said they'd send it right out as soon as it was compiled."

Kelly glanced at his watch. "That's just half an hour from now."

When Blake heard the report from Washington, he wrote it down and handed it to Kelly.

"Weather conditions propitious for a Friday morning start," Kelly read. "Saturday conditions will be less favorable."

Kelly called Mac right away. "Mac, have you got your passage booked for New York?"

"I've got my ticket," answered Mac. "What's the word?"

"Weather's okay, we start in the morning. You better get over here right away."

Concealing his excitement, Mac returned to the banquet and quietly excused himself. An abundance of rumors and abortive takeoffs had left him reluctant to announce another possible false alarm. The duck diners would learn from the next morning's newspapers that their speaker of the night before was halfway across the continent.

On Friday morning, Kelly and Mac awoke at quarter to four and ate a hearty breakfast at a nearby cafe. By five, armed with their 20 chicken sandwiches and several packs of cigarettes provided by the restaurant owner, they arrived at Rockwell Field where, in the pre-dawn darkness, the shadowy figures could barely be discerned in the eerie yellow glow of searchlights. Newsmen appeared at the field despite the early hour.

The moon was still visible over Point Loma, as Kelly told Mac, "Looks like it's going to be our kind of day."

"It not only looks like it, it's definitely going to be," Mac stated positively.

✺

At daybreak, on November 3, 1922, the two fliers took their respective places in the T-2 for their second attempt. After several minutes of warm-up, the mechanics pulled the chocks from the wheels. The monoplane rolled down the runway and finally climbed out into the clear air. Banking around in a wide circle about a mile offshore, the aircraft steadily gained altitude until, as it soared over Rockwell Field ten minutes later, it had picked up 800 feet of altitude with a groundspeed of almost 60 mph.

Their flight plan would take them through the Temecula Pass and over to Tucson by following the Southern Pacific Railroad tracks. From Tucson, they would turn east to Tucumcari, New Mexico, turn north through Oklahoma to Wichita, St. Louis, Indianapolis, Dayton, and over Pittsburgh to Mitchell Field on Long Island.

The T-2 flew safely over the pass at an altitude of 2,000 feet, clearing the highest peak with a safety margin of nearly 800 feet.

Mac had taken over in the front cockpit as they crossed the Colorado River at 8:51 a.m., a little less than three hours out of San Diego. As he neared Tucson, he began struggling to keep the fragile line between a maximum climb and a stall, which would allow him to fly over the high mountains surrounding the desert town. The T-2 was at its ceiling, 2,900 feet, traveling at 92 mph, the engine turning at 1,520 rpm, but as each obstacle loomed ahead, he worried whether the plane would clear it.

The air was rough and turbulent, with updrafts suddenly lifting the aircraft 300 feet, then just as suddenly dropping it down again, putting a terrific strain on the pilot. Often, with a peak looming straight ahead, Mac felt certain that they would slam right into it, only to have an air current catch the plane just before the collision and fling it up and over. For long periods, the T-2 was barely 40 or 50 feet above the Arizona desert, with Mac struggling to maintain even that minimal altitude.

Soon after passing Tucson, Mac discovered a small water leak in the number-two cylinder. The loss of coolant worried him. By noon, they had passed over the Dragoon Mountains of Arizona with 400 feet of altitude, but strong winds continued to buffet the plane from the southwest, which, though lessening fuel consumption, made control difficult. Mac's arms ached from the long hours of struggling with the stick. His shift continued over Bowie, Arizona, into Deming, New Mexico, where, a half-hour later, he was glad to hand over the forward controls to Kelly.

Then, Kelly took his turn battling the elements. Near Tecolote, New Mexico, downdrafts caused by the Great Divide forced the giant plane to within 20 feet of the ground, barely missing sagebrush, scrub trees, and an occasional jackrabbit. The T-2 skimmed along barely 150 feet above the mountain tops. For miles, Kelly worried that he would crash into the ground.

Although the two pilots tried to follow their original course over the high elevations north of the Rio Grande River, they quickly realized that continuing on this course would eventually force the plane right into the ground. Hastily, Mac and Kelly passed notes back and forth and decided to veer southward through a little valley parallel to the San Andres Mountains, which would use more gasoline to lighten the plane, but would enable it to climb over the 8,900-foot range. After several attempts to make it over the slopes, they finally cruised above the crest with 50 feet to spare.

As night closed in, Kelly headed north through the ancient Malpals lava beds, which stretched for 80 to 100 miles, around Carrizozo, New Mexico. The low-flying plane elicited considerable consternation and amazement among the colorfully robed Indians going about their normal evening routine. The sight of this huge aircraft (or any aircraft, for that matter) seemingly headed straight for them, just 50 feet overhead, sent them diving headlong into their caves and mud huts.

Low clouds had moved in around 5:00 p.m., obscuring horizontal visibility. Kelly attempted to follow the silvery ribbon of railroad tracks winding through the desert, but soon lost them in the total darkness of night. He struggled to keep the plane headed toward the east/northeast without a fixed point from which to determine his position. Because his mariner's compass was probably about ten degrees off, he could only head in a general direction.

As they swung northward, Kelly passed a note back to Mac: "If we could reach Tucumcari, we'd know where we are and could start from a known point for the long night ahead." After spotting lights a few minutes later, Mac passed a note up to Kelly: "I see lights ahead, maybe that's Tucumcari."

Weather conditions were bad and getting worse, the clouds so low that the T-2 occasionally flew straight through them. Now and then, the moon peeped out from between the scattered clouds, offering a quick view of the terrain and making piloting easier as the men traveled over the Texas and Oklahoma panhandles. At midnight, they were over the Canadian River, a distinct landmark that snaked through the country below.

But the weather report had failed to mention a violent thunderstorm over Kansas, into whose vortex the big monoplane plunged. Piercingly cold winds, driving rains, and brilliant lightning unmercifully buffeted the T-2. Sitting out in the open air, Mac was soaked to the skin in a matter of minutes and nearly frozen.

The steady roar of the Liberty engine sweeping through the skies overhead startled many slumbering families on the plains of Oklahoma and Kansas. Awakened from a deep sleep, they jumped to their windows to see the huge aircraft, a dark ghostly shape spurting fire from its exhaust stacks, pass out of view into the stormy night. The next day, newspapers reported that a tornado had passed over Kansas that night, killing 12 people and injuring 80!

As the T-2 tossed about in the turbulent skies like a raft on choppy seas, Mac began to wonder why he had ever wanted to attempt such a foolish journey.

The aircraft had no radio, so the pilots could not communicate with anyone on the ground. When the sound of the engine roared over larger cities, the Associated Press alerted San Diego that the pilots were adhering closely to their planned schedule. Over sparsely populated areas, the telegraph wires remained silent.

Brilliant red-orange sunrays rising against a cloud-speckled sky appeared shortly after the T-2 passed over the lights of St. Louis. Because the depletion of fuel had made the plane lighter and because the storm and the long night had passed, the pilots' spirits rose. Mac sent a note up to Kelly, who was then in the front cockpit, in the jovial spirit of the morning: "Nice work Kelly, old boy. What do you want for supper tonight at the Waldorf Astoria?"

But his optimism was premature, for shortly after he passed his note, serious trouble started.

Although Mac and Kelly had first noticed the cracked cylinder as the T-2 passed Tucson, they had been too absorbed in the troubles of the long stormy night to think about it. But as they had continued on over the western plains of Kansas and over Missouri and Illinois, several cracks had formed in the cylinder jackets and water began leaking from both sides of the radiator, spurting out in ever-increasing amounts over the engine and, to a lesser degree, over the pilot himself. The engine temperature had risen to dangerous levels.

In a desperate effort to cool down the engine and continue the flight, the pilots began pouring into it every liquid they could find — the remains of the consommé, the coffee, and their drinking water. But the liquid spurted out faster than they could pour it in. About 50 miles beyond Indianapolis, with the engine temperature gauge indicating 110 degrees, Mac banked the big ship up on one wing and flew to the Indianapolis Speedway for an emergency landing, sick at heart that after all they had been through, and just when it began to look as if they could actually make it, engine trouble had thwarted their flight.

As the fliers approached the track at an altitude of 3,000 feet, Mac decided they could make it to Schoen Field at Fort Benjamin Harrison, near Indianapolis, which was a better-equipped facility. Throttling back, he pushed the stick forward and nosed the T-2 down in a shallow glide toward the military field. As the plane crossed the threshold of the field, he cut the power, and the propeller froze. A dense cloud of white smoke poured from the engine. As soon as the T-2 stopped rolling, Mac and Kelly leaped and ran, putting as much distance as possible between themselves and the aircraft before it exploded. Fortunately, it never did.

◈

Although their second flight had established a new world's distance record, their third within a month, the media chose to ignore this fact and instead reported the pilots' use of unorthodox coolants, dubbing this the "Soup Flight."

The two pilots left the T-2 at Fort Benjamin Harrison and, borrowing a plane, flew back to McCook, keenly disappointed over the failure of their trip. Mac later explained,

> When Kelly and I jumped out of the T-2 at Indianapolis, we didn't do much talking about transcontinental non-stop flights. We were through, finished. Anyone who wanted our job and was foolish enough to take it could have it. And although neither of us said much, it was pretty well settled in our minds that this type of flying was a good thing to keep away from if we wanted to stay healthy.

Their attitude was short-lived, because the two men began discussing plans for a third trip almost immediately after their return to McCook Field. They visited one afternoon in Mac's McCook office, acknowledging that each time they had attempted the non-stop flight, they had had trouble getting over the western mountain ranges because of their heavy fuel load. "What about checking to see if there is any time during the year when the winds blow the other way, east to west, so we could fly in that direction?" Mac asked. "By the time we'd get to the high mountains in the West, we'd have a much lighter fuel load and more climb power."

Mac and Kelly decided to check with the weather forecaster in Washington and they learned that during the last two weeks of every April, a peculiar weather condition known as a Hudson Bay High reversed cross-continental wind flow. One to three of these reversals occurred each year.

The two aviators were elated, for this new information might allow their flight to succeed. Getting in touch with General Patrick again, they outlined the new weather information. He listened carefully, asked a few questions, and before he hung up, said he would think it over.

◈

Because their endurance record at San Diego was still being contested by the French, the two erstwhile cross-country fliers decided to break the record again — this time with enough officials, certified instruments, and observers to satisfy any skeptic.

As Mac and Kelly climbed into the Fokker T-2 for another attempt at breaking the world's endurance record, the mayor and many other leading citizens of Dayton assembled at the field to wish them "Godspeed." Movie cameras rolled. The pilots waved to the crowd as they rolled down the runway, only to become hopelessly and ignominiously mired up to their wheel hubs in the deep mud at the end of the field.

Several days later, when the ground was thoroughly frozen, the pilots conducted another endurance attempt, but with less publicity. The plane with an experimental Liberty-12 high-compression engine took off at 4:00 p.m.

Kelly and Mac flew a measured triangular course that took them about 20 miles away from Dayton. Kelly flew the first six hours, and Mac flew the next six. During the second shift, an excessive pre-ignition developed in the new engine. It sputtered, faltered, and finally quit altogether. The pilots had started their original endurance flight at San Diego, because they had been worried about landing the T-2 with a heavy load of fuel. Now, in total darkness, in a blinding snowstorm that dropped temperatures to 8 degrees, without landing lights, with approximately the same fuel load as they had had at San Diego, and with a dead engine, Mac and Kelly decided to land.

Pointing the monoplane's nose in the general direction of the field and toward a light on top of a building, Mac lowered the nose for a landing, expecting to crash into the ground. The violent crash never came, yet a sharp jolt caught the aircraft as the wheels touched down. The impact nearly knocked the plane over on its side, but it finally righted itself. Except for a leak in the oil line, neither the T-2 nor the pilots had suffered any damage. They had stayed in the air for over eight hours before being forced down, but the flight set no record.

Undaunted, the fliers made another attempt on April 16, 1923. This time Orville Wright, representing the Aero Club of America, the U.S. affiliate of the *Fédération Aéronautique Internationale*, served as an official observer, with Otis Porter, also of the Aero Club, serving as a timer. Five or six officials took shifts of eight hours each as observers. The Fokker T-2, with a Liberty-12 standard compression engine substituted for the experimental high-compression engine, was loaded to capacity with gasoline. Mac and Kelly waited in the plane, with the engine warming up and propellers rotating evenly, but they couldn't start their flight because Wright was late.

Kelly, who was in the front cockpit for the first shift, suddenly closed down the engine, leaned out over the side of the cockpit, and yelled, "Where's Wright? Where's that damn Wright?" That "damn Wright" came hurrying up just in time to hear Kelly's remarks. Kelly waved a sheepish hello.

Wright made every effort to conform with the rules and regulations of the *Fédération Aéronautique Internationale*. A triangular 50 kilometer course was laid out, with a pylon at each of the three points of the course. The water tower at Wilbur Wright Field became the home pylon; the McCook Field water tower served as another. A point near the village of New Carlyle served as the third. Official timers positioned themselves at each pylon, standing their eight-hour shifts in the cold and rain.

Slowly the big plane rolled down the field, gradually gaining altitude until, flying at 1,000 feet, it circled the field past the timing stand at 9:51 a.m. The T-2 completed its initial lap, the fastest of the 81 laps flown, in less than 22 minutes. During succeeding laps, the time drew out to 29 minutes. The average speed that first day was 80 mph, but as the fuel load lessened, so did the speed at which the aircraft could be kept aloft, and it was slowed to 70 mph. Throughout the next two days, the Liberty engine droned over Dayton as the T-2 continued its steady course around the pylons.

Around 5:00 p.m. on the second day, the pilots dropped a note down indicating that they would land between 9:00 and 10:00 p.m. that night.

Because of their close proximity to the engine, the instruments regularly smudged over with smoke and grease. Kelly wiped them off with his handkerchief several times while he was piloting the plane. At one point, after cleaning the instrument glass, he noticed that the battery indicator was registering discharge. As he watched, it slowly returned to its normal position. This happened several times just after Kelly wiped the glass. He was just about to send a note back to Mac in alarm, when he realized that the static electricity in his silk handkerchief was causing the problem.

Night settled over Dayton once more, and the beacons came on to light the way. At 9:45 p.m., the men circled the field for a landing. Veteran aviators, watching as Mac brought the plane down, said the landing was one of the prettiest sights they had ever seen. The darkness was intense, and the T-2's lights had burned out, so only the steady hum of the engine gave any indication of the plane's whereabouts.

Searchlights, one on the wind vane and another flashing fitfully in an effort to keep the T-2 in its beam, bathed the glide slope as the silhouette of the plane settled softy to the ground, with perfect precision. Automobile headlights closed in about the field from every direction, and the din of cheers, shouts, whistles, and auto horns drowned out the signal pistols announcing the moment of landing to the timers. Throwing open the cabin door, Kelly shouted enthusiastically, "Gosh Mac, this is bigger than San Diego!"

☙

The flight signified the most to Orville Wright, for it had taken place at the very spot where he and his brother had made their first seconds-long flights. Now, almost 20 years later, a huge plane, with 10,850 pounds of weight, had remained in the air continuously for more than 36 hours. Wright's struggle against apathy, indifference, and his dedication to and belief in the future of aviation were vindicated.

General Patrick, highly pleased with the new world record, sent his personal congratulations to the two airmen and his official permission to make another attempt at a transcontinental non-stop flight whenever they were ready.

To the surprise of everyone on the base, Kelly and Mac reported for work as usual the next morning, apparently little affected by their lack of sleep or their achievement.

The endurance record resulted in a special victory for Mac, who now held the world's altitude, endurance, and distance records simultaneously. He would receive the Mackay Trophy — awarded annually for the most outstanding achievement in aviation — three times, a record never yet equaled.

. . . As the T-2 flew . . . toward the Pacific Coast, it gobbled up fuel . . . a mixed blessing, for the plane needed a lighter load to climb over the approaching mountain ranges, yet enough to remain aloft for the remainder of the journey.

Chapter 5

Coast-to-Coast, Hours Twelve to Fifteen

In the Thick of the Night

THE SKIES HAD BEEN MISTY all around Dayton on May 2nd, 1923. But as the T-2 crossed into Indiana, the clouds thickened and the black of night intensified. Flying at only 800 feet, Mac searched through the murk for the lights of Indianapolis, as the propeller whipped icy winds across his unprotected face. Once past the city, he followed the glimpses of car headlights traveling the highway to Terre Haute. When the town was directly below, he glanced at his watch and saw that the time was 7:30 p.m. Mac hated to leave the warm, friendly glow of civilization for the menacing black that awaited him to the west.

Cruising along through the darkness at 90 mph, Mac saw a dim flicker of light on the propeller. At first, he thought the flicker came from Kelly using his flashlight to see if the siphon was leaking. But it grew into a large, ghostly white ball appearing and vanishing in the mist. Mac had no idea where the light came from, and it worried him.

Then they hit rain, falling softly at first, but as they flew deeper into the clouds, it turned into a torrent, dripping down the neck of Mac's uniform and fogging his goggles. With no lights to follow below, he relied solely on his instruments. When the airspeed became too great, he knew the T-2's nose was pointing downward; but when it slowed, with the nose pointing upward, the plane might stall. When the compass swung, the plane was turning; but with no fixed points to watch outside, he had trouble knowing how many turns he had made.

After Mac had been flying for several hours, he sighted another mysterious shaft of light coming from the countryside below. It broke through the clouds at regular intervals, swinging from the left to the right as its reflection returned to the ground. He wondered if he was looking at the searchlight from Scott Field in Belleville, Illinois. Mac had heard that the local pilots had planned to wire a searchlight to the top of a dirigible hangar. If he was right, then he could be sure that the T-2 was on course. He was so relieved when Kelly passed a note to him asking, "Do you think that could be the Scott Field searchlight to the left?" that he banked the plane toward the friendly beacon.

On the ground, pilots and engineers aimed the searchlight toward the sound of the engine, catching the T-2 as it shot out of the clouds. The beacon swung ahead of the plane, indicating its proper westerly course. To express his gratitude, Mac tossed three red flares over the side.

The rain continued, forcing Mac to drop to 400 feet and to pray that no tall, unlighted structures lay in his path. In the gloom, every minute felt like an eternity.

At 10:15 p.m., another glow eventually appeared to the west, and became increasingly brighter until it lit the entire cloud-filled sky. Mac cheered to himself. The lights belonged to Jefferson City, Missouri, and indicated that they were right on course.

Press reports and newsreels later quoted a Kansas City policeman who had heard a powerful roar overhead as he was walking his beat around midnight. He detailed how he had seen the big monoplane fly past in the darkness with fire spurting from its exhaust stacks. Railroad employees working just north of the city claimed to have heard a powerful plane traveling "at a high rate of speed" across the Missouri River. They felt certain it was the T-2. Yet, these reports were mysterious because Mac and Kelly never flew closer than 75 miles to the south of Kansas City.

After seemingly endless hours of flying through the rain and darkness, the T-2 finally burst through the clouds into a star-studded sky. For the first time in over five hours, Mac began to relax. He looked at his watch; his shift was over. So he waggled the stick and crawled back through the tunnel to the rear cabin.

Although exhausted from his six-hour battle with the weather, he couldn't sleep. His mind raced with thoughts about his work, what he was now attempting, and what he might do in the future. Instead of reclining on the bench, he stared through the window at the spectacular countryside below. As they flew over the Kansas plains south of Wichita, he watched the Arkansas River glisten in the moonlight.

Mac had not eaten for six hours, so he picked up the Thermos and poured himself a piping hot cup of consommé. The sweet steam sent a wonderful rush of warmth through his body, for he was still soaked and cold from his night in the rain. The menu never changed on these long flights, but to a ravenous pilot, the standards tasted like a gourmet meal. After feasting on his soup, Mac unwrapped a cold chicken sandwich and devoured it, savoring every bite; then he devoured another. From another Thermos he poured himself a cup of coffee. That the caffeine would keep him awake presented no problem, for he knew that sleeping would be impossible anyway.

As the T-2 flew over the fields and plains of Kansas toward the Pacific Coast, it gobbled up fuel as greedily as its pilot had taken down his soup and sandwiches. The rapid fuel consumption was a mixed blessing, for the plane needed a lighter load to climb over the approaching mountain ranges, yet enough to remain aloft for the remainder of the journey.

With the arrival of dawn, the fields of Kansas appeared to have merged with the buttes and eroded topography of New Mexico. The warm early light intensified the landscape's spectacular pastel hues. Mac casually watched the strange formation of the earth below until he noticed small cubes arranged with unusual regularity. Wondering what marvel of nature had caused such a peculiar design, he soon realized that he was looking at the adobe huts of Indians. "We're in New Mexico!" he shouted. "There's the graveyard at Tucumcari."

Spotting the graveyard, the first recognizable landmark he had seen in hours, meant that the T-2 was right on course after flying through darkness for hundreds of miles. Although it was a welcome sight, he couldn't help but wonder about its possible symbolism.

The Other Side of Heroism — Life as an Experimental Pilot

Although Mac's career as an experimental pilot was thrilling, it sometimes hindered his social life. Being young, handsome, charming, and famous, he was a frequent guest of prominent citizens in Dayton, San Diego, and other cities in which he worked.

But, aviation in the 1920s was a strange and dangerous occupation. Every time a daring pilot soared into the sky behind a buzzing propeller, he risked returning to earth with a sickening thud. Such a groom represented a dangerous gamble to a young lady with hopes for a long and happy marriage.

In 1921, while Mac was testing the MB-3, a new biplane, in Ithaca, New York, he met a pretty, 19-year-old named Molly at a dinner party given by her parents. She was petite, with short, curly brown hair, dimpled cheeks, and lovely brown eyes — a young lady who knew she had a subtle power over men. Mac was captivated but cautious, wondering if someone so young could be serious about anything. But as the evening wore on and they moved from dinner to a country club dance, she took a more serious tone with him. When his body pressed against hers as they danced, long-suppressed feelings surged within him — Scotsmen are good at suppressing their emotions! Excited by her acceptance of a dinner date for the next night, he walked home as if drifting through the air.

Mac picked up Molly around six, in a car furnished by the Thomas Morse Company, builder of the MB-3. He found her parents in the living room enjoying a drink before dinner and accepted their invitation to join them, though, because of his profession and his mother's influence, he rarely imbibed. In this case, he wanted to be sociable and to relax. So, he fielded their questions about aviation — this unusual mode of transportation introduced a few years earlier by the Wright brothers — until Molly strolled down the staircase and entered the living room. Her face flushed as she took his hand in greeting. As usual, he attempted to hide his emotions.

During dinner Molly forced him to open up and talk about himself. Reluctantly, Mac told her about his background, his years at Stanford, his stint as an amateur boxer, and how he had become involved with airplanes.

The evening had gone too quickly, and Molly realized that she should be leaving. Back at home, at the front door, she held out her hand in a shy goodnight. Mac wanted to hold more than her hand but was afraid he'd ruin the whole relationship if he rushed her.

"When can I see you again?" Mac asked. "I don't have much time here in Ithaca. How about tomorrow night?"

"Tomorrow night" it would be, at six.

From then on, Molly and Mac saw each other every night.

Mac had come to Ithaca to test the Thomas Moore MB-3's maneuverability as a combat pursuit airplane. One day, while trying out the aircraft at 10,000 feet, he heard a terrible crash and felt the plane jerk. Suspecting that the propeller had broken and crashed into the wing, he looked out of the cockpit and saw that most of the wing fabric had torn away, leaving the webs and woodwork bare. With no fabric left on the wing, the plane had no lift.

Mac wished he had been wearing a parachute, so he would have a better chance of surviving the crash. As the plane dove toward the ground, he cut the ignition switches to prevent the 40 gallons of gasoline and himself from bursting into flames. He threw his arms over his face and head to protect them against the guns and instruments and pulled his legs to his chest. "I'm a dead man," he told himself.

When the MB-3 hit the ground, the landing gear and the tail crumpled. The fuselage bounced high in the air, turned a complete somersault, and landed on its back. Mac was pinned under the plane.

Students and faculty from nearby Cornell University campus ran to the wreckage, sure that the pilot was either dead or fatally injured. As they managed to lift the debris off of Mac, he crawled out under his own power, stood up, and did a few calisthenics to make sure no bones were broken. The spectators sent up a loud cheer.

When Molly saw Mac that night, she had already heard about the crash. Her apprehension over his future flights was evident.

But Mac held her tight, stroking her hair, glad for the opportunity to comfort her in his arms. "You don't have to worry," he reassured her. "When I fly I do a lot of thinking ahead about what to do in case of an emergency just like this one. If you plan ahead for any emergency, you can usually get out without too much damage." But he knew that his reassurance was what he called "pure baloney," said only to make her feel better.

Luckily, he had only suffered a few cuts and bruises in the crash of the MB-3, but he was as likely as any other pilot to meet an early end. He had never before considered how his career would impact a romantic relationship, but when Mac and Molly said good-bye, he was aware of her fears for his and their future.

On leave while waiting for the MB-3 to be repaired, Mac flew to Los Angeles. He took a taxi to his parents' house from the airport thinking that he would surprise them. He gave the taxi driver the Carondelet Street address and sat back to enjoy L.A.'s familiar nighttime sights and sounds. Closing his eyes, he drifted off to sleep, when suddenly he was jolted awake by the sound of the driver's voice.

"This what you're looking for, mister?" the driver asked. "Looks like a vacant lot to me."

Mac looked up, stunned. "Are you sure we're at the right address?"

"This is the right address. But there ain't no house here now," the driver replied.

Mac called his parents, and his mother's sleepy voice answered.

"Oh, John," she said. "I'm so sorry. We thought you would call before you came. We moved the whole house a few days ago. It was a sudden decision. We're at 300 N. Plymouth Boulevard, right on the corner of Plymouth and Beverly — bigger lot, nicer area."

Then as an afterthought, she added, "By the way, dear, just so you don't get any more surprises, we have Laura Turner's daughter, Nelliejay, visiting for a little while. I'm sure you'll enjoy meeting her. Now hurry on over, we can't wait to see you."

Walking up the unfamiliar path to the familiar house, Mac found his mother and father waiting for him at the door, clad in their bathrobes. Although normally undemonstrative, his parents took turns dispensing hugs and kisses, for they hadn't seen him in several years.

The next morning, Mac and Ben, his father, were out on the front lawn talking after breakfast, enjoying the warm sunshine and balmy air, unaware that they were being scrutinized from a second-floor window. Priscilla curtains blowing gently in the breeze hid the viewer from their sight.

Nelliejay Turner, the daughter and only child of one of Mattie's dearest friends, was the house guest Mattie had mentioned the night before. She was a pretty, vivacious, 24-year-old. Her fresh complexion and large blue eyes had set many a young man's heart pounding at Ohio State University, where she had been a member of the Kappa Alpha Theta sorority. Petite and dainty, with a fine full figure, she was one of the most popular girls in the Theta house — known for her brains, charm, and good looks. Yet after a couple of years of college, Nelliejay had grown bored and quit school, going to work for a friend as hostess at the Miramar Restaurant in Columbus. She was spending her short vacation with the Macreadys.

Nelliejay watched Mac from the window. She had heard about him from her mother and read about him in the newspaper. She wondered what she should say. How do you talk to a flier? "How's the weather up there? Had any good crackups recently?" Well, she thought, he sure was cuter than he appeared in his picture.

Shortly after her arrival at the Macready's, Mattie had showed her a framed photograph. With a straight face, Mattie said, "I wonder if you've ever met my son?" Nelliejay looked at the picture and choked back a gasp. It showed a man in a flying suit, a mask with a long tube running out of its nose covering his entire face and head. He looked more like a monkey than a man.

The pangs of hunger reminded Nelliejay that she hadn't yet eaten breakfast. So with a hasty glance in the mirror, she left the window and went downstairs. The rest of the family had long since finished their breakfast, the kitchen had been cleaned, and all the food had been put away.

Rummaging in the refrigerator, Nelliejay found a plate of cold corn-on-the-cob, from the previous night's dinner. After adding some salt and butter, her breakfast was complete. She was leaning over the sink, chomping away on the cold buttery corn, when Mattie and Mac entered the room. Years later, Mac remembered the scene well.

"Nelliejay," Mattie said. "We've been looking for you. I want you to meet my son, John."

"Nice to meet you," Mac said, formally. But his eyes twinkled in amusement at Nelliejay's obvious dismay at being caught with corn kernels smeared across her cheeks.

"I'm pleased to meet you, too," she mumbled. "I thought I could sneak down here and get something before anyone came."

"Is this your breakfast?" he asked.

"Well, yes, cold corn-on-the-cob is my favorite," she answered as she prepared to finish her treat.

"That's the darndest thing I ever heard of. Don't you eat regular breakfast food?" Mac asked.

"Oh sure, but not when there's cold corn."

After her winning first impression, Nelliejay didn't see Mac for the rest of the day. So, she was surprised when he asked her to go to a movie that evening after dinner. For the following two weeks, as their friendship developed, Molly progressively disappeared from Mac's thoughts, until she was forgotten.

Mac took Nelliejay for long walks, to dinner, to the theater, and for excursions into the countryside by automobile, yet they were never alone.

Then just as suddenly as their holiday together began, it ended when Mac received a telegram informing him that his roommate at McCook Field, Pat Moriarity, had died in a plane wreck. Mac left immediately, promising Nelliejay he would write. Mattie took him to the station, asking a very disappointed Nelliejay to wait at home for an expected package.

The next few days were difficult for Mac; Pat had no close living relatives, so the burden of making funeral arrangements, of gathering personal effects, and of seeing to legal responsibilities, fell on Mac's shoulders.

When he had settled all of Pat's affairs, he plunged himself into his work with renewed vigor, hoping to forget his sorrow. He wrote long descriptive letters to Nelliejay daily. For the first time in his life, he became an avid correspondent. Naturally shy, Mac had always found direct communication difficult — a trait that would plague him all his life, affecting his relationships with friends, business acquaintances, and even his family. But writing was a different matter, and he poured out his thoughts, feelings, hopes, and fears on paper. He wrote of his work, of the planes he flew, of the men he worked with, of amusing anecdotes and events, though he never mentioned the dangers and the deaths.

Nelliejay answered in kind, and their intimacy grew.

In October 1922, before the second coast-to-coast attempt, while Mac was waiting for the T-2 to undergo some much-needed repairs in San Diego, he sent Nelliejay a wire in which he asked her to meet him for dinner the following day at a well-known downtown restaurant in Los Angeles. When she read the message, she felt her heart skip a beat at the thought of finally being alone with him. She knew Mac's family would not be pleased — young ladies were never alone with young men — but after some gentle, persistent persuasion, she had her way. She did, however, agree to accept Ben Macready's offer to accompany her as far as the restaurant.

Over dinner at a candlelit table for two, Mac and Nelliejay remained oblivious of the diners around them, some of whom began to recognize Mac from his picture in the newspapers.

Mac and Nelliejay talked for hours that night. He watched her as she chattered away, her eyes properly averted. After several hours, she looked at her watch and was surprised by the time.

"Come on," he said, a slight sense of urgency in his voice. "Let's get out of here."

Mac got up, pulled her chair out, and helped her on with her coat. He paid the bill, and they walked outside in the chilly October night to catch a streetcar home, for by then she was living with his parents.

When the streetcar arrived, the couple walked to the little platform outside where they could be alone. At the back of the nearly deserted car, he pulled her close, wrapped her in his arms, and tenderly kissed her. As the trolley rattled and bumped along the rails, Mac asked Nelliejay to be his wife. He wanted to get married immediately after he completed the long-planned-for transcontinental flight. Her ready acceptance earned her another squeeze and hug.

The next morning, the family was gathered in the spacious dining room for a breakfast from the buffet loaded with platters of ham, scrambled eggs, English muffins, marmalade, bacon, browned potatoes, and large crystal bowls of fresh hothouse strawberries. Mac announced his engagement to Nelliejay. Everyone started talking at once, congratulating them both, asking about their wedding plans.

A few days later Mac returned to San Diego, for he received word that the T-2 had been repaired and that they would soon be on their way for another try at the coast-to-coast flight. A long, worrisome wait had begun for Nelliejay.

. . . Mac saw that he was flying at 10,000 feet. . . . He continued trav-eling to the west, hoping that he wouldn't end up in a box canyon of high, sheer rock walls that would prevent him from turning the plane around.

Chapter 6

Coast-to-Coast, Hour Seventeen

As the Earth Rose into the Sky

OVER SANTA ROSA, NEW MEXICO, Mac once again took the front seat. Heading through a winding and irregular pass leading toward the summit of a rapidly rising slope, the T-2 flew over the muddy thread of the Rio Grande River as it flowed across the barren volcanic landscape. Mac and Kelly were searching for the lowest route to Phoenix. They had intended to fly due west to a point about 20 miles south of St. Johns, Arizona, and, from there, to change to a southwesterly heading to avoid the high-est terrain.

Mac had followed the lowest topography that his contour maps indicated, believing that this course would take the plane over steadily rising terrain until finally reaching a precipice, then dropping down to Phoenix. However, as he passed St. Johns, he found himself over the lowest point of an enormous plateau. The ground elevation in the direction of their intended course was much higher than their present position; the T-2 was already at its maximum ceiling.

Glancing at the altimeter, Mac saw that he was flying at 10,000 feet. To the southwest, he could see a gradual upslope leading to peaks covered in some blackish material he assumed was lava. Calculating that the heavy aircraft could never climb that high, he continued traveling to the west, hoping that he wouldn't end up in a box canyon of high, sheer rock walls that would prevent him from turning the plane around.

Below, sharp cinder cones poked up through the black lava beds; flat-topped mesas revealed their pink and gray strata. After flying over the picturesqué formations for a while, Mac turned sharply toward the south, hoping to find a pass — the way out.

Joe Stiff — Parachuting in the Dark

"Joe Stiff" was a funny little man who wore a drab olive uniform and a perpetual grin. Although pilots tossed him from bomb-bay and cabin doors at high altitudes, in a spin, or with just a few hundred feet between him and the ground, he never uttered a word of protest. When something went wrong, he hit the ground with a dull thud.

Joe was a rope-and-sandbag dummy built to test a recent invention — the parachute.

Pilots at McCook Field, who considered themselves fearless, resisted wearing parachutes because they felt that strapping on the newfangled "contraption" indicated that they didn't expect to bring their planes down in one piece.

"You're not going to wear *that* thing?" pilots would ask anyone they caught harnessing up.

A single tragedy changed their attitude.

On March 13, 1922 — a cold, clear, windy day — Mac had asked Lieutenant F. W. "Neidy" Neidermeyer if he'd like to go up for some combat practice. "I see your favorite plane just came down."

Always eager for a mock dogfight, Neidy replied, "You bet."

"Don't forget your 'chute," Mac said.

But Neidy had already pushed halfway through the pilot's room door. "Oh, hell. I'm not going to bother with it this time."

After the two pilots had climbed into their planes and taken off into the skies above the field, an appreciative audience of engineers, secretaries, pilots, and mechanics gathered outside to watch the aeronautic ballet. The planes spun, looped, dove, climbed, and darted over and under each other in an effort to gain tactical advantage. The contest had been going on for a few minutes when Neidy's MB-3 pursuit plane suddenly pulled away and leveled off, trailing a stream of paper-like white confetti. For no apparent reason, flakes of wood, and then entire chunks of wing fabric peeled away from the plane and floated off into the sky.

Neidy frantically struggled to gain command of his aircraft, but the disintegrating control surfaces left him no way to maneuver.

As the onlookers watched in horror, the MB-3 spiraled out of control until it crashed with an impact that tore up clods of dirt and sent debris in every direction. When the remnants of Neidy's plane finally came to a rest, the air field fell deadly silent.

On March 29, the commanding officer of McCook Field issued the order that every flier "shall wear a parachute on every flight from this field from this date on."

Seven months later, in October 1922, test pilot Harold Harris climbed into his cockpit to prepare for another dogfight. Within a few seconds, he climbed back out and called to the timekeeper. "I need another 'chute," he said. "I had a new seat cushion installed yesterday and it makes the harness too tight."

But the new parachute proved to be even tighter than the first. Harris didn't want to delay his flight any longer, because Muir Fairchild, his designated opponent, had already taken off and was now circling the air field. So he said, "Never mind, hell, I'll just go without one," and started back to his plane. But mindful of the March 29 order, he turned around, grabbed his original parachute, and climbed back into the cockpit. With a few turns of the prop, the engine caught, and he followed Fairchild into the air.

Harris caught up to him over North Dayton, where they simulated firing their forward guns by flying directly at each other. As Fairchild veered off to one side, Harris closed in on his tail. They were about a half-mile from downtown Dayton when, after following Fairchild's gradual left turn,

Harris's plane began to shake violently and its stick began to oscillate wildly between his knees. Although he recognized the problem — the plane's newly installed experimental ailerons were out of balance — the only thing he could do was decelerate as quickly as possible. Harris pulled the throttle back, but his efforts came too late. The aileron whip had torn the wing structure apart and was forcing the stick to oscillate 1,000 times a minute, beating his right hand until it became limp and useless.

Harris had never made a parachute jump before, but, figuring that now would be as good a time as any to give it a try, he crawled out onto the wing. As soon as he pulled himself from the cockpit, the force of the wind blew him off the wing and stole any chance he had to hesitate.

Locating what he thought was the release ring and cursing himself for not paying attention during training sessions, Harris pulled it three times before he realized that it belonged to his leg strap. When he found the proper ring, he yanked it hard, and out floated the most beautiful sight he had ever seen — a cloud of billowing white silk.

After recovering from his emergency exit, Harris noticed that he was dropping into a grape arbor. A concerned farmer, who had spotted the descending pilot, ran to help him and arrived just as Harris crashed, landing directly on top of the farmer. Neither man sustained any serious injuries, but Harris did ruin his favorite pair of pants.

For making the world's first emergency parachute jump, Harris became the charter member of the Caterpillar Club — an informal organization of those individuals whose lives had been saved by a parachute.

Above: John A. Macready is pictured with his parents, Mattie Delahunt Beck Macready and Benjamin Macready, in front of their home in Los Angeles, California, after the successful non-stop flight across the United States, in 1923.

Left: Enlistment picture of John A. Macready when he joined the U.S. Air Service, in 1918, at Reno, Nevada.

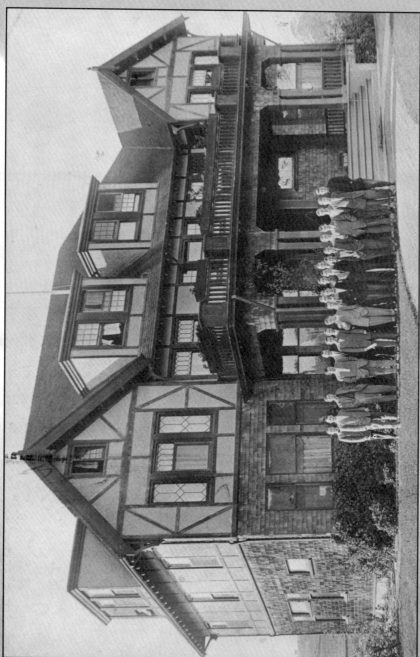

The Kappa Alpha Fraternity House at Stanford University, Palo Alto, California. John A. Macready was a member during his undergraduate years. Some years later, he became president of the Alumnae Association. Macready is second from left.

The Quartette Mine, Searchlight, Nevada, one of the largest producing gold mines in the state, was discovered by John A. Macready's father, Benjamin Macready, and produced over $9,000,000 net during the late 1800s and early 1900s. John Macready was elected Justice of the Peace of Searchlight at the age of 25.

View of McCook Field, Dayton, Ohio, in the 1920s, showing runway and its proximity to the Miami River. Many a pilot ended up in the river if he miscalculated his landing roll, since airplanes at that time had no brakes.

Test pilots of the U.S. Army Air Service, 1920s, McCook Field, Dayton, Ohio. From left, back row: Lieutenant Johnson; Lieutenant Hoy Barksdale; Lieutenant John A. Macready, chief test pilot; Lieutenant Hutchinson; Lieutenant Moffett; Mr. Louis Meister; Mr. R. G. Lockwood; Lieutenant Tourtellot; Lieutenant James Doolittle; Lieutenant Amis. Shown with their "dumbbell trophies" (for pulling a stupid "boner" like test-flying the wrong airplane) awarded when warranted.

The largest plane ever built during the 1920s, the six-engine Barling Bomber, 42,000 pounds loaded, proved awkward and cumbersome to fly. Macready, on one test flight, had all six engines go dead at once but brought the plane down safely in the pasture that was known as Wilbur Wright Field.

John A. Macready, in the DeHavilland biplane over a Catalpa Grove in the first successful aerial crop-dusting, Troy, Ohio, August 1921. Witnessing the event below are Department of Agriculture representatives.

John A. Macready in his leather flying suit, cap, and goggles, with the ten instruments for recording data onto smoked paper on his high-altitude flight. The instruments were placed in the DH-4's rear cockpit and sealed by the official observers prior to takeoff.

Chief test pilot of the U.S. Army Air Service John A. "Mac" Macready, suited up for high-altitude test flight. In spite of all the layers of clothing, the -80 degree F temperatures, plus the wind chill factor of the open cockpit, made the pilot bitterly cold.

Standing in front of the high-altitude Le Pére biplane are, left to right: Lieutenant John A. Macready, chief test pilot; Dr. Sanford Moss, inventor of the supercharger; Colonel Thurman H. Bane, commanding officer of McCook Field; and Adolph Berger, chief mechanic. Note the supercharger mounted on the engine right above the propeller.

Page opposite: The specially built oversized propeller mounted on the Le Pére high-altitude biplane. Note the supercharger right above the propeller. This prop was designed to counteract the problem of an earlier prop that had spun off Macready's plane due to lack of air pressure at high altitudes.

Left: Inside the cockpit of the Le Pére high-altitude test plane. The round object (left) is the mirror that reflected the outside air temperature (OAT) from the wing-mounted thermometer. The knob on side of cockpit (lower left) is for the supercharger. Macready's experimental test work was classified, thus little was known about it at the time.

One of the experiments to combat the lack of pressure at high altitudes included this "pressurized cockpit." The pilot was supposed to see out of the little round plate glass window, which proved inadequate, and climb through the 22-inch round, solid steel door. It proved to be more like a metal coffin.

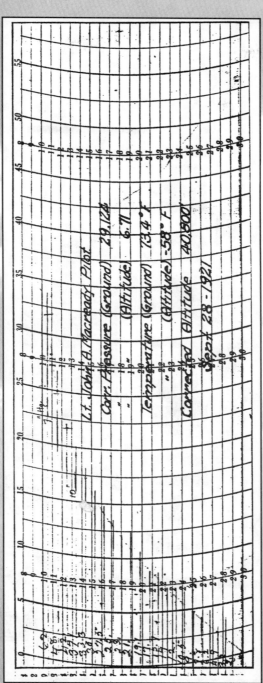

A photograph of the barograph chart showing the high-altitude of 40,800 feet reached by John A. Macready in an open cockpit plane.

The *Paper That Does* ngs.

Dayton Evening Herald

DAYTON, OHIO, THURSDAY, SEPTEMBER 29, 1921.

rs tonight, cooler;
and cooler.

KILLED IN TWO HU

LT. MACREADY AWAKENS TO FIND HIMSELF FAMOUS AS HOLDER OF ALTITUDE RECORD

Here's Smile He Got Eight Miles in Air

FLOODED BY WIRES OF CONGRATULATION UPON HIS SUCCESS

Many Offers Made to Buy
Written Story of Record-
Breaking Flight.

The *Dayton Evening Herald's* front page announced Macready's world-altitude record. He wrote his own story in the *National Geographic* magazine.

The famous Fokker T-2 which made the first non-stop flight across the United States, is shown between the Thomas Morse MB-3 (l) and the Sperry Verville Racer (r), illustrating the imposing size of the T-2. The "T" stands for transport.

The Thomas Morse MB-3 biplane, with test pilot Macready in front, at the scene of the crackup near the campus of Cornell University, Ithaca, New York, during the 1921 test flight of the combat pursuit plane. Macready crawled out unscathed.

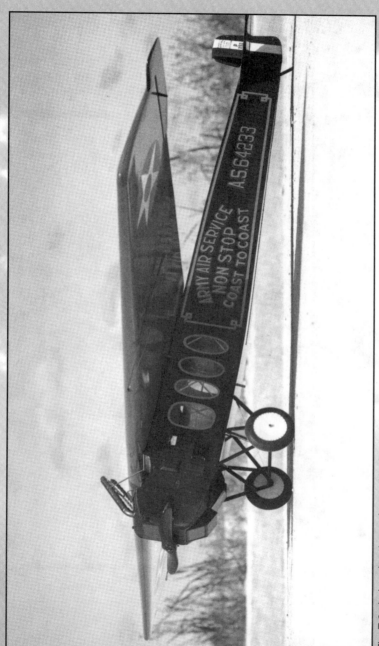

The T-2, designed and manufactured by Fokker, with a steel-tube fuselage and a full cantilever wooden wing. Lieutenants Oakley G. Kelly and John A. Macready flew the plane 2,470 miles on May 2-3, 1923, at a ground speed of 92.05 mph, in 26 hours and 50 minutes.

The T-2 and its pilots, John A. Macready and Oakley G. Kelly.

John A. Macready and Oakley G. Kelly on the non-stop transcontinental flight.

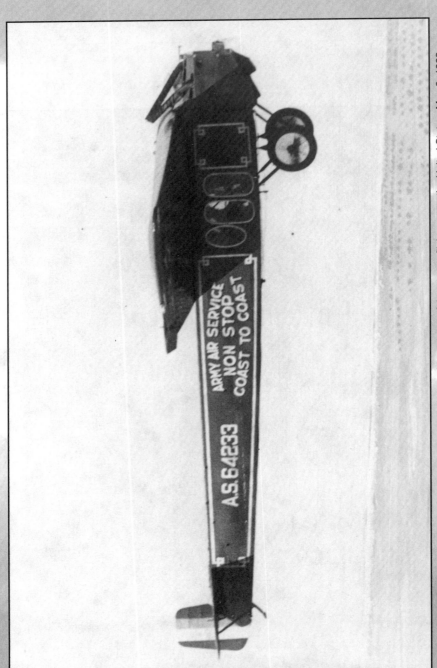

The Fokker T-2 transport approaching San Diego on its final leg of the successful non-stop flight across the United States, May 3, 1923.

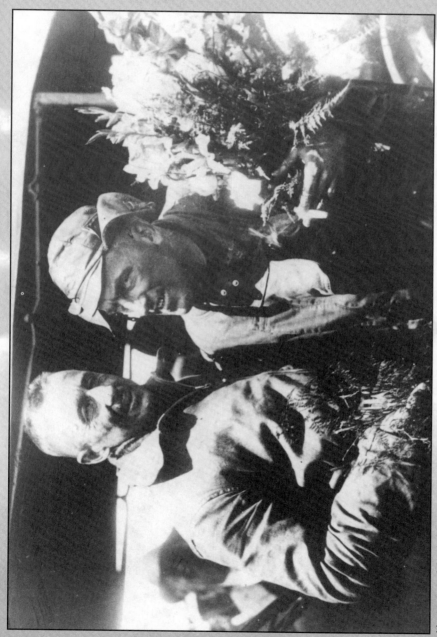

Lieutenants John A. Macready (l) and Oakley G. Kelly (r), greasy-faced and begrimed with exhaust fumes, receive flowers and accolades upon landing after the first successful non-stop flight across the United States in 1923, at San Diego, California.

Nelliejay Turner Macready, wife of John A. Macready. They were married May 9, 1923.

Nelliejay Macready, in the cockpit, was the first civilian woman to be allowed a flight in a military airplane. Husband John, standing in front, of course, was the pilot.

A good view of the supercharger mounted on the side of the fuselage of the specially built high-altitude XCO-5 biplane

Left to right:
John A. Macready, chief test pilot;
Adolph Berger, chief mechanic;
and an unidentified civilian.

The Loening Amphibian COA AS 24-8, built by Grover Loening, and considered as the plane for the Macready/Doolittle transPacific flight in 1925. (This plane can be seen at the U.S. Air Force Museum, in Dayton, Ohio.)

The first aerial survey in the DeHavilland 4B (DH-4B). John A. Macready is in the front cockpit; A. W. Stevens is in the rear.

A. W. Stevens (in plane) and John A. Macready (standing by wing) with the DeHavilland DH-4B used for the first aerial photo survey of America.

Aviation history is well summarized in the careers of the three pilots shown above: in the cockpit is Colonel Charles A. Lindbergh; beside the plane (l. to r.): Brigadier General Gilmore; Lieutenant John A. Macready, holder of the altitude, endurance and distance records; and Orville Wright, co-inventor of the Wright Flyer that made the first powered flight in 1903, at Dayton, Ohio, after Lindbergh's flight across the Atlantic in 1927.

A banquet honoring Orville Wright at Dayton, Ohio. Wright is seated under the American flagpole, head table. Macready is four persons to the right. A model of the Wright Flyer is displayed in back of Orville Wright.

John A. Macready in Washington, D.C., 1973, receiving special honors as the only three-time winner of the Mackay Trophy. He presented the Mackay Trophy to the winner at the ceremonies that same year. The Mackay Trophy is awarded annually for the most outstanding achievement of the year.

The Mackay Trophy, symbol of excellence in aviation and awarded annually by the National Aeronautical Association, is on display at the Air and Space Museum in Washington, D.C.

. . . Hoping to conclude their trip in less than 27 hours, Mac made one turn over North Island to head into the wind and touched down at 11:26 a.m. Eastern time, exactly 26 hours and 50 minutes after taking off from New York. . . .

Chapter 7

Coast-to-Coast, Hours Twenty, Twenty-Six — and Destination

A S THE T-2 APPROACHED THE BLACK MASS Mac had thought was a lava bed, he discovered that it was, instead, a forest of tall green pine trees. The sight was mesmerizing and he nearly flew straight into the forest before realizing what he was doing. Banking the large plane hard to the right, he managed to avoid the tops of the tallest trees. The T-2 would never climb over the forest, so Mac flew alongside the dense growth, which was broken occasionally by little rivulets or the sparkling glint of a waterfall.

After paralleling the woods for more than 80 miles, he was beginning to feel hopeless that they would ever reach Phoenix. Then the hoped-for opening appeared in the higher ground to the south, and Mac, with a feeling of relief, eased the stick to the left, turning the big monoplane through the pass.

The scene that greeted Mac as he flew through the canyon and out into the open country made his heart sink, however, for instead of finding the Salt River Valley he had hoped to discover, there was nothing but more canyons and ravines rimmed on all sides by high, sharp volcanic peaks.

"One of these canyons has to lead to Phoenix," he told himself. "Suppose we follow one of these mountain-rimmed canyons and find it's a dead end?"

Mac decided to fly due west by the compass for the Pacific Coast and prayed that following this path would not prove futile. He flew the T-2 across the lowest ranges by following the ravines and eventually crossed over another set of mountains. Once on the other side, the Arizona desert spread out before him with all its stark, rock-strewn desolation. To Mac, it could not have looked more beautiful.

The Smithsonian Institution's *Annals of Flight* series (volume 1, number 1) in describing Mac's flight, notes that at 6:00 a.m., the men were over Santa Rosa, New Mexico, 1,725 miles into the journey, average speed 93.75 mph. At 9:30 a.m., Mac and Kelly were over Show Low, in eastern Arizona, 2,035 miles into their flight, and 10,000 feet above sea level.

At mile 2,210, the men checked their position on the map at Wickenburg, in western Arizona. They crossed the Colorado River, between California and Arizona, at mile 2,320.

After crossing the California Valley, Mac and Kelly spotted the city of San Diego due west, shimmering in the morning sunlight, 8,000 feet below. The pilots felt elated that they had made it all the way to California and were relieved that their grueling flight was over. But they also felt slightly annoyed that, despite their life-risking adventure through the storm-swept skies of America, San Diegans were going about their business while unaware of the historic event taking place above their heads.

Mac and Kelly had no way of knowing that the whole nation had been glued to its radio sets while following the progress of the T-2 and its pilots.

The nation's interest caught up to them when the airmen finally came down over the city, where the news of their arrival had preceded them. Mac and Kelly were astonished when military escorts from Rockwell Field and North Island appeared on both sides of the T-2. They were amazed to see 100,000 San Diegans rushing through the streets and across rooftops, waving anything they could get their hands on as Mac brought the big aircraft down to just 100 feet above the city's tallest buildings. In their excitement, men tossed their jackets from the tops of buildings and beat their straw hats to a pulp against railings.

As prearranged with Kelly, Mac had moved to the cockpit, to have the honor of landing the aircraft.

Hoping to conclude their trip in less than 27 hours, Mac made one turn over North Island to head into the wind and touched down at 11:26 a.m. Eastern time, exactly 26 hours and 50 minutes after taking off from New York — a journey so short that the coffee in their Thermos bottles was still warm! As the T-2 settled smoothly down to earth in a graceful landing, a mighty chorus of sirens, horns, and whistles swelled to a crescendo from every corner of the city. From the harbor, Naval ships added their blasts to the pandemonium.

As Mac climbed from the cockpit, his face splotched with oil and grease from the Liberty engine, the swelling crowd swept the guards aside like so much chaff and with wild yells surrounded the grinning fliers. Showering them with bouquets of flowers, they lifted the pilots onto shoulders and paraded them around the air field in triumph.

Through the army of press photographers, Mac caught sight of Nellie-jay standing by a hangar at the fringes of the jubilant crowd. When he offered her a helpless and grease-smeared smile, she blew him a congratulatory kiss.

After the successful record-breaking flight, Mac and Kelly received many telegrams. President Warren Harding wrote: "You have written a new chapter in the triumphs of American aviation." General Patrick offered congratulations on the successful completion of their flight, as did Ezra Meeker of New York City, who wrote:

Congratulations on your wonderful flight, which beats my time made seventy-one years ago by ox team at two miles an hour, five months along the way. Happy to see in my ninety-third year so great a transformation in methods of travel. Ready to go with you next time.

Colonel Franklin R. Kenney, who had watched the T-2's hair-raising takeoff from Long Island and, with more faith than conviction, had bet on the flight's outcome, sent this message through another Air Service officer:

I win five thousand dollars if Macready and Kelly are successful in nonstop flight. Will you wire, my expense, Macready and Kelly asking them if they will accept the five thousand as a gift to celebrate with their wives the greatest achievement in our aviation history? You explain to them and make the gallant young bull pups take it.

The two "young bull pups" thought Kenney was joking, but after being convinced of the offer's authenticity, Mac and Kelly sent this reply:

To do anything that needs doing is a soldier's plain duty, but when the accomplishment brings victory to a friend, it makes it a pleasure. With grateful acceptance of your magnificent gift there is a satisfaction in the knowledge that it pays to bet on the Army Air Service.

Although neither of the pilots mentioned it to Colonel Kenny, one of the reasons the $5,000 was so welcome was that it helped to pay the personal expenses of the two men. The remuneration they had received from the government for the flight was but a small part of the actual money Mac and Kelly had to spend in order to make the flight successful. Had they not won the money, they both would have gone considerably in debt over this enterprise. This non-stop transcontinental flight proved the feasibility of and gave tremendous impetus to commercial aviation.

. . . Like many men in hazardous occupations, the test pilots were a highly superstitious group. They refused to walk under ladders; they avoided black cats.

Chapter 8

Down to Earth
— Post Flight

FTER MAC'S SUCCESSFUL FLIGHT ON MAY 2-3, Nelliejay set May 9th, as the date for the wedding. Unfortunately, that day also was the hottest day Los Angeles had experienced in 18 years. The air was close, humid, and stifling; flowers wilted, hairdos sagged, and tempers flared.

The wedding was meant to be a small, quiet affair at the spacious Macready home. But from early morning on, newsmen, photographers, and newsreel cameramen surrounded the house, jockeying for position, pushing, shoving, and snapping photos of everyone who entered or exited.

Mattie had been busy for days supervising the servants in making the house ready. They cleaned the house from top to bottom, washed windows until they sparkled, polished silver to a butler's patina, cleaned upholstery, and waxed floors. Great tubs of orange blossoms flanked the wide staircase as well as the altar, their soft fragrance permeating the entire house. Jasmine leaves twined gracefully through the white latticework of the altar at the foot of the wide stairway.

Nelliejay wore Mattie's white, sleeveless wedding dress of stiff heavy satin, with a wide, oval neckline, simple fitted bodice, and flared, waltz-length skirt appliquéed with a soft green and pink flower motif. A short white tulle veil covered her soft chestnut curls. Unfortunately, the suffocatingly hot day transformed her tight curls into limp, damp tendrils, necessitating a last minute "fix" with a cornmeal wash by her hairdresser.

Nelliejay had insisted on having lilies of the valley for her bridal bouquet. What normally would have been a simple request became a nightmare, because no florist in the city could find her the flowers. Just when she was about to give up hope, some friends, who had heard of the emergency, picked some from their own garden. The flowers were hastily arranged to encircle the small white Bible she carried, cascading gracefully over its sides.

Mac was a "basket case." The man who considered risking his life a normal part of a day's work had never been so nervous before. When he stepped to the mirror and took hold of his tie, he discovered that his hands were shaking too much to make a knot. Eventually, he called his best man, Oakley Kelly, to come and help.

Radiant in her white satin dress, flowers strewn through her glossy hair, Nelliejay paused on the landing to take her mother's arm before turning to face the guests and proceeding down the stairway, a shy smile spreading across her face. As she reached the bottom step, Mac stepped up and gently took Nelliejay's arm.

As Reverend Charles Thompson pronounced them husband and wife, Mac lifted the veil from Nelliejay's face and, for the one moment in his life during which he forgot his shyness, brought her to him in a lengthy kiss. The onlookers cheered and applauded joyously.

Shortly after cutting the cake with Mac's engraved military sword,

Nelliejay slipped upstairs and changed into her traveling outfit. Together, they drove to San Diego for their honeymoon at the Hotel del Coronado.

Despite attempts to keep their honeymoon plans secret, the newspaper photographers found them, plaguing them with the pop of flashbulbs and requests for autographs. Mac and Nelliejay had little privacy even in their own room, for the bellhop, who had known Mac at McCook Field, constantly dropped by on one pretext or another. They did manage to sneak away to Catalina Island for a few days, and upon their return, they went to the U. S. Grant Hotel. There Mac introduced Nelliejay to one of his idiosyncrasies.

A few days after their return from Catalina, Nelliejay was shopping in downtown San Diego and saw a dress she "simply had to have." She asked Mac about buying it, and he replied, "Sure, by all means, go ahead."

When they returned to the hotel, she modeled the dress for him. He liked it so much he wanted her "to go back and see if you can get another just like it." Mac believed that if one is good, more is better, and he practiced this philosophy all his life, filling his attic with bags, trunks, and boxes of duplicate items that he had "liked and stocked up on" but had never used.

Following the May 2-3 transcontinental flight, the Air Service relaxed its policy prohibiting wives from flying in military aircraft. Nelliejay was the first wife to take advantage of this change.

On Sunday morning, May 20, 1923, she waited for her first trip in the T-2 while standing in a receiving line at Rockwell Field with Mac, Kelly, Secretary of War John W. Weeks, and a party of senators and congressmen who had gathered for a special ceremony. Unaware that she would be enclosed in the plane's cabin, Nelliejay had bundled up in layers of sweaters, a jacket, and a coat, as if for a trip to the North Pole. As she shook hands with the 5,000 passing guests, the heat and the excitement of the occasion overwhelmed her, and she fainted, collapsing into the arms of the Secretary of War.

On the following Thursday, Mac and Kelly planned to start ferrying the T-2 back to Washington, D.C., making public-relations stops along the way at El Paso, Texas; Lawton, Oklahoma; Kansas City and St. Louis, Missouri; as well as Dayton. Nelliejay would follow by train.

But before they left, the new bride pulled a mammoth housekeeping error. Because flying the T-2 placed pilots out in the cold, they wore long woolen underwear beneath their uniforms. Mac had only two sets of this vital apparel. On Wednesday night, Nelliejay washed out both sets of his underwear by hand, with the noble intention of sending her new husband off with nice clean woollies. But she had completely forgotten about the cold foggy San Diego night air — and mechanical dryers were unknown at the time. The underwear was still cold and wet when Mac dressed the next morning. His trip to El Paso was, naturally, extremely uncomfortable.

In Dayton, Nelliejay found herself in a fast-paced routine full of military protocol and official, private, and civilian parties. During their first year of marriage, they moved three times as she required ever-increasing room to entertain. Because Mac often brought one or two of his buddies home for lunch without notice, she developed the habit of having plenty of soup and sandwiches on hand — a state of readiness she maintained for the rest of her life.

To have some time alone, Mac and Nellie would turn out all the lights in the house after dinner, go upstairs to the sun porch, and pretend they were out when the doorbell started ringing. But callers always left their small white formal cards, requiring, according to the custom of the day, that the visits be returned. Some evenings, they would go out early, only to return to the ubiquitous calling cards left at their door.

Like many men in hazardous occupations, the test pilots were a highly superstitious group. They refused to walk under ladders; they avoided black cats. One evening, Lieutenants Wendell Brookley, Hoy Barksdale, and Lester Maitland dropped by the Macready house for a drink on their way home. Nelliejay busily fixed tasty tidbits and rounded up ashtrays, while Mac and his guests chatted in the solarium. She brought in a tray of drinks and placed the canapés on the table within easy reach. Then, seeing the three pilots pull out their cigarettes for a smoke, she found matches and began lighting their cigarettes for them. She had two lit and was preparing to light the third, all on the same match, when Barksdale jerked his cigarette away. She looked up in surprise as everyone fell silent.

"Nelliejay, you never, ever light three cigarettes on one match," Mac said.

Mac's and Nelliejay's first dinner guests were Judge and Mrs. Clark. Nelliejay had gone to great pains to provide a sumptuous repast, which included a large roast chicken surrounded by rosettes of mashed potatoes squeezed through a pastry tube. The platter resembled the finest dish from a fancy restaurant. But Mac looked at it in dismay, wondering "how the hell" he was going to carve that bird and keep those little potato rosettes on the platter at the same time. The arrangement was tight. Gamely, he picked up the knife and started to carve, while three pairs of eyes followed his efforts in fascinated anticipation.

Acutely aware of her husband's discomfort, Nelliejay started an animated conversation with the Clarks, hoping to distract them. Sticking the fork into the chicken's breast to keep it steady, Mac cut down through the leg where it joined the body, slowly at first, then with increasing pressure. But just as he started to bear down, the fork slipped, the knife hit a bone, and the entire chicken, potato rosettes and all, slid off the platter into the Judge's lap.

The newlyweds "misadventures" continued, with Sam, Mac's Airedale puppy and the brother of President Warren G. Harding's dog. Sam was an integral member of the Macready household. When, on one occasion, Anthony Fokker, the Dutch aircraft designer, was the Macreadys' dinner guest, Sam was resting comfortably in the kitchen with the cook, patiently waiting for the scraps he knew would be coming his way when the plates were cleared. He was not disappointed, for after the cook carried the plates through the swinging door separating the kitchen and dining room, she scraped the remains into his dish. He dove into them with great gusto, noisily chomping, gnawing, and scraping. The noises that accompanied his gastronomic delight were so loud that Fokker, who was sitting in the dining room, declared, "Aha, sounds like someone is eating in the kitchen!" The remark became a refrain in the Macready household for many years thereafter.

Some two years later, in November 1925, Anthony Fokker returned to Dayton to bring his highly touted new transport plane, a larger version of the T-2 (Fokker IV), for performance testing by the U.S. Air Service. During his stay, Fokker was again a guest in the Macready home. At dinner one evening, with the conversation naturally gravitating to aviation, Nelliejay casually mentioned that she had only been up in a plane once or twice in her life, due to the strict Air Service regulations. Fokker turned to her with just a trace of a smile on his lips and asked, "How would you like to go for a ride in my new transport plane?"

Nelliejay was delighted. Fokker pulled out his "little brown book," thumbed through it, and asked, "How about tomorrow?"

"Oh, dear," Nelliejay answered, "I can't tomorrow, I'm having my bridge club here," she said, her voice trailing off in disappointment.

Fokker was silent for a moment, then suggested, "Well, that's all right, why don't you bring them along?"

Nelliejay was overwhelmed.

The next day, as the ladies assembled for lunch, Nelliejay announced the afternoon's entertainment. A chorus of excitement responded to the news, mixed with a bit of anxiety on the part of several who had never been up in an airplane before. However, no one wanted to be left out.

When the party arrived at the field, Fokker greeted each one individually. He had a small ladder brought out to aid the ladies in climbing up into the cabin. Standing at the door, he offered a helping hand as they stepped aboard. Just prior to takeoff, when they were all seated, Fokker brought their pilot back for an introduction. Much to Nelliejay's surprise, it was Mac!

Once airborne, Fokker added a festive note to the affair by passing around a five-pound box of fine chocolates. Without a doubt, this special day and Anthony Fokker's gracious friendliness significantly enhanced Nelliejay's standing among the ladies of the bridge club.

As the young Macready family grew — with two-year-old Jo-Anne and a second daughter on the way — Mac and Nelliejay decided to buy their own home, a two-story frame house in the secluded Hills and Dales section of Dayton. They also purchased a large Doberman Pinscher, which they sent to obedience school for training as a watchdog. Because of

Mac's growing fame and his frequent trips out of town, they feared that their children would become an inviting target for the curious — even kid-nappers. Some years later, in 1932, the kidnaping and death of aviator Charles Lindbergh's 20-month-old son proved that their caution had been well-founded.

. . . The area over which they flew was entirely uncharted. . . . Clouds swirled and billowed around the peak as they approached, gradually reaching higher around the mountain until finally, while the biplane was still a few miles away, the summit disappeared from view.

Chapter 9

A Bird's-Eye View — Photographing America from the Air

O N AUGUST 1923, three months after the triumphant non-stop flight, General Mason M. Patrick selected Mac to accompany Captain A. W. Stevens, the Air Service's official photographer, to Ensenada, Mexico, where they would take the first high-altitude pictures of a solar eclipse.

Elated over the assignment, the two fliers requested and were granted permission to leave a month before the eclipse and to photograph points of interest en route to Ensenada in a DeHavilland DH-4B. Packing a few changes of underwear and their toothbrushes, they took off from Dayton on August 23, 1923.

The first leg of the Macready-Stevens photographic expedition took them to North Platte, Nebraska, with stops in Iowa City, Iowa, and Omaha, Nebraska, along the way. They arrived in North Platte just about noon, circling the field and shooting several photographs before landing.

Once on the ground, the fliers went into town for an "aviator's lunch." According to Mac, the meal consisted of a thick juicy steak — "the kind that cost two dollars or more in New York" — veggies, potatoes, gravy, and bread and butter, all for "four bits." With the exception of the DH-4B and the two-dollar per diem provided by the Air Service, the two men paid their own expenses, and thus, a good cheap meal was a real bonus.

From North Platte, Mac and Stevens flew into Cheyenne, Wyoming, where they spent the night. On the next leg, they flew to Rock Springs, Wyoming, where they refueled before going on to Pocatello, Idaho, their main base for operations in Yellowstone National Park. Because Mac was unfamiliar with the topography around Pocatello, he had contacted a friend, Harry McDougal, who had been an ace during World War I, and had become one of Pocatello's leading attorneys.

Mac asked McDougal to mark a potential landing spot. But when they arrived, they had trouble finding McDougal's marker. Mac and Stevens flew for ten miles up and down the valley looking over all possible sites, finding nothing that looked feasible.

Finally, near a railroad-tie treating plant, the airmen discovered a cloth "T" marking a field that had formerly been used for an aerial circus and that had since been considerably cut up by deep ditches across which not even an automobile could drive. The DH-4B had no brakes and, therefore, might roll right into one of the ditches. But because it was the only location with any landing potential, Mac decided to take the biplane down there anyway.

Mac circled several times, then pulled the power back as he approached the "field" to land. The plane was at minimum flying speed as he "dragged" it in low on final approach. Keeping the nose straight ahead to avoid ground looping, Mac cut the power off to stall the brakeless plane on to the ground, to minimize rollout. The plane slowed to a stop in a smooth area in one corner of the field.

At the time, Pocatello was a small town where an airplane landing attracted a lot of attention. The citizens turned out *en masse* to greet the two fliers, happy to round up the proper fuel and to find volunteers to

guard the aircraft overnight. (From previous experience, Mac knew that
the plane would have been cannibalized by morning if it went un-
guarded.)

The next day, McDougal invited Mac and Stevens to explain their
predicament — how to take off on such a rutted field — at a meeting of
the local Chamber of Commerce. Mac used all his persuasive abilities to
convince the locals that the field, in which they took such great pride, was
actually a trap from which the DH-4B would be unable to take off. His
speech succeeded, for, after a day's delay, a crowd of public-spirited citizens arrived at the field accompanied by a tractor, a scraper, four horses,
and a plow.

Mac wrote in his log:

> We wielded shovels and filled badger holes and ditches impar-
> tially, finally the work of burning off the sagebrush and filling
> in the ditches was completed, and we were ready to leave for
> Yellowstone.

After a delay of several days caused by bad weather, Mac and Stevens
took off and crossed the Blackfoot and Caribou Ranges of Idaho into
Wyoming. Mac's log describes their attempt to photograph Yellowstone
National Park:

> We follow north the general direction of the river forming the
> lake's outlet and in about ten minutes are in sight of the Grand
> Canyon of the Yellowstone. At the head of the canyon, the Yel-
> lowstone River leaps over the Upper Fall, over a hundred feet in
> height, and a half mile lower down it drops a sheer three hun-
> dred feet to the bottom of the canyon. The coloring is spectac-
> ular. Bright orange, yellow, red, and purple hues predominate
> and are set off very effectively against the dark green pines with
> which the margins of the canyon are fringed and the white foam
> of the river at the bottom of the chasm. We fly the length of the
> canyon, seeing a view no man has ever seen before, making
> exposures as we go, then circle and come back low over Obser-
> vatory Peak, waving our hands at the autoists who stop their

cars in the middle of the road to watch in astonishment the first airplane to fly over Yellowstone Park — too surprised to even wave back!

We had planned on going to the Mammoth Hot Springs, but a single look at the sinister black clouds filling the spaces between the mountains to the north convinced us it would be useless to attempt photography. The storm had already broken in the distance, and we were beginning to wonder if we had not already lingered too long in this beautiful but strange region.

The next morning Mac and Stevens left for Boise, Idaho, where they would headquarter for a couple of days while photographing Mount Rainier, Mount Adams, and the Columbia River, in the state of Washington. Mac's log describes their landing:

We fly over the Capitol, cross the river, and make after some rapidly moving clouds of dust in the desert, which we know are caused by our friends on the ground who are breaking the speed limits to get to the flying field before we do and watch the landing. It is a close race, for although we have more speed, they know where they're going and have a good start. As we settle to a landing on the desert, the first auto rolls up and out jumps Senator Whitten with a bucket containing cracked ice and something that looks like beer. It proves to be only the one-half of one percent variety, but never, even in the old days when real Budweiser was procurable, did a beverage prove more satisfying, for our throats are in the condition technically known as "cracked." Hoisting our bottles high in salute, our pictures are taken and later appear in the evening paper with the caption, "Above the Three Mile Limit." An elderly lady, devoted to the church, afterward saw this picture and earnestly remarked: "I do hope you boys were not really drinking!"

Early the next morning Mac and Stevens took off for Vancouver, Washington, where they landed, hastily refueled, and, without waiting to grab a bite to eat, due to impending bad weather, started back in the direction of Mount Rainier. Gaining altitude, the airmen could see that ominous dark clouds had completely obscured the sky. They would be attempting to photograph sharply rising mountain peaks while flying blind through clouds, and would be relying on hoped-for openings in order to come out on top. As Mac noted in his logbook:

> We now do quite a foolish thing, for although we are approaching mountainous country, we go up through the clouds until we are a few hundred feet above them and completely out of sight of the ground.

The area over which they flew was entirely uncharted. Flying by compass, Mac headed in the general direction of Mount Rainier, while Stevens managed a few exposures of the cloud formations. In a few moments, they could make out the great dome of the mountain thrusting up through the cloud layers. Clouds swirled and billowed around the peak as they approached, gradually reaching higher around the mountain until finally, while the biplane was still a few miles away, the summit disappeared from view.

Their situation was critical, because their sole landmark and the topography below had vanished. Diving down through the cloud layers in this mountainous country would have been suicide. Mac looked around, trying to figure out "what the hell" to do, while making a slow 360-degree turn. He could barely see the edge of the cloud mass far off to the southeast — or at least what he thought was the edge. So he attempted to out-race the wind to the leading edge of the storm. Behind the men the clouds churned, boiling up in great cumulous towers, layer upon layer. Lightning streaked across the sky in blinding flashes, and thunder rumbled through the heavens.

Mac wrote in his logbook:

> Our engine is running well and brings us in less than a half-hour over a point east of Mount Adams, where we find we are just ahead of the clouds. The summit of Adams is shrouded in vapor and banks of fog are pushing around its sides and over the top. We make some exposures of the enshrouded summit and

the glacier-covered slopes, and in this brief time the clouds are swirling around us again.

Spotting a good-sized opening in the clouds below, Mac spiraled the DH-4B down through it, and came out over the forested hills in the direction of Mount Hood, finally landing safely at Vancouver, Washington.

Although the flight had been dangerous and stressful, Stevens had taken some startling photographs of the cloud-covered peaks, none of which had been photographed before. After spending the night in Vancouver, the airmen refueled the DeHavilland, and took off to photograph the Columbia River and surrounding points of interest.

⚅

On September 4, 1923, Mac and Stevens headed south through California, stopping overnight in Redding and Sacramento. They photographed Yosemite National Park before proceeding to Los Angeles, where they spent three days photographing the city and visiting family and friends before continuing on to San Diego, five days later.

On Saturday, September 10, Mac and Stevens took off from San Diego's Rockwell Field en route to Ensenada, skirting the coast of Southern California just beneath a heavy bank of fog, which made this an unpropitious day for aerial photography. They prayed that the cloud layer was thin enough to contain some holes through which they could climb.

The fog appeared to be lifting as the fliers approached Ensenada. Holes opened in the cloud layer at 5,000 feet, so Mac pushed the DeHavilland up through until it came out on top, only to discover a second layer of clouds. He maintained the biplane's steady climb and, at 14,000 feet, penetrated the lower limits of this second layer. Punching up through the fleecy mist, he could see nothing surrounding him but a white wall. Without an outside reference point or instruments on which to rely, Mac did his best to maintain the two-ton plane's orientation. Light rain drenched his goggles and ran back over the wing surfaces in little rivulets, trailing off in a thin sheet of water.

The DH-4B was still struggling to break through the cloud layer at 16,000 feet when the moon eclipsed the sun. The light waned for a moment. Then, the leading edge of the moon's shadow passed over them. Later, Mac described the scene:

Outside the fuselage, long blue flames writhed from our exhaust pipes; it was like a flight at night in every way, except that there was a horizontal band of color wherever we looked. To the northwest, this band was a wonderful red and orange; to the southeast, it was white. As the shadows passed on, the band became rose-colored in all directions, and after a few moments the northwest became white, while the southeast turned red. Then, as suddenly as it had come, the shadow whisked on by us.

Stevens, who was hanging out over the side of the DeHavilland, snapped pictures in rapid succession. The photographs, though good, weren't spectacular, and their superiority to any others attempted that day — notwithstanding claims by the Navy to the contrary — failed to make the two aviators feel better about their mission.

Before heading back to Dayton, Mac and Stevens made a series of photographic forays around the Los Angeles area, taking the first aerial photographs of Mount Wilson, Santa Monica, Hollywood, and various sections of the city itself. Then they took off for Las Vegas. On their way, they detoured to circle Mount Whitney, in Southern California, where they snapped the first photographs of that snow-capped mountain peak.

Over Death Valley they spotted the small, nearly extinct mining town of Skiddoo, which was perched several thousand feet above the valley on a barren slope. Only a half-dozen small buildings remained; prospectors and miners had removed the others, one by one, to remoter locations in adjacent canyons.

The heat was intense and oppressive, even at their altitude. As they overflew the area, Mac recalled the town's legend of a rugged mining prospector, who had lived in the smallest and hottest of these shacks. He finally died and found himself in Hell, as the story went. After the devil assigned him to miserable quarters, the prospector stood the climatic conditions as long as he could . . . but finally gave up and asked his friends topside for some blankets!

As the heat waves shimmered over the parched and baked desert below, the hot blasts of air lent some measure of credence to the tale.

ॐ

When Mac and Stevens landed in Las Vegas, a contingent from Searchlight greeted them, including an old friend named Pete Klegal, who had waited for Mac at a local tavern. Klegal was in an expansive mood as he rushed over, giving Mac a handshake that nearly broke his wrist. "Good ta see ya, Mac ole fren', ole fren'. Here," Klegal said. "I want ya ta have thish." He pulled a ring topped with a huge gold nugget from his finger and thrust it into Mac's hand.

"Oh, no. No, Pete. I couldn't take that. Here, you take this back," Mac said.

"No! No! I inshist you keep it, I wan ya ta have it. It's from the Searchlight Quartette Mine." Klegal pushed the ring away.

Whether in a more sober moment Klegal ever regretted his action, Mac never learned. But he treasured the ring and the friendship of the man who gave it to him.

ॐ

During the following day, September 20, Mac and Stevens spent nearly five hours photographing the Colorado River Reclamation Project. Later, they circled over Las Vegas to get pictures of the city, before landing and spending another night there.

Early the next morning they took off for the Grand Canyon. As Mac dropped the plane down into the canyon, then pulled the stick back and swooped straight up the steep walls again, Stevens took some spectacular photographs.

Doing some fancy flying, Mac attempted to give Stevens the best position from which to do his work. Often in the bumpy, hot air of summer, turbulence would buffet and toss the DH-4B so severely that both men would lift off their seats. Only their safety belts kept them from being tossed out. Stevens had the more dangerous job, for many times to get a good photograph, he had to unstrap his safety belt, stand up, and lean over the side of the plane as Mac banked it in a 60-degree turn. Stevens' sole link to the aircraft would be a broad strap of tough tape that he had fastened to a belt around his waist. Stevens easily lost himself in capturing the magnificence of a scene and sometimes forgot about the danger as he reached out over the fuselage with his camera. A sudden jar would make him lose his balance and force him to withdraw into the cockpit. Then he would turn to his pilot and yell, "Go around again, Mac, will you, so I can get another shot." Mac always obliged.

⁓❧⁓

Their next photographic destination was Holbrook, Arizona. Arizona is occasionally host to some spectacular electrical storms during the summer and early fall. One of the fiercest of these storms had preceded the DeHavilland's arrival, leaving the desert drenched and flooded. Streams and dry washes suddenly turned into raging, foam-crested torrents of water.

As Mac guided the biplane over the desert floor, he saw water everywhere he looked and had no way of determining the depth. He passed a note back to Stevens that read: "Keep your eyes out for a white sheet spread on the ground. That will be our landing field." Another friend had marked the spot.

Mac searched for the marker. And when he spotted the sheet, it looked like a pocket handkerchief, and the "field" looked no bigger. He knew he could never land there, so he pulled back on the stick to gain altitude for a better vantage point, flying in ever-widening circles, searching for a flat, dry spot in the flooded desert. So much rain had fallen in such a short period of time that the land below looked like a series of small lakes, each connected to the other, with the giant saguaros, multi-branched ocotillos, and chollas poking up through the water like swimmers.

After glancing at the fuel gauge, which indicated that the tank was empty, Mac knew he would have to land regardless of the conditions. He looked for a spot that would do the least damage to the DH-4B.

Mac headed back north of town to an area that had looked impossible when he had first flown over it. A quick "drag" of the area confirmed the worst of his fears to be true — the aircraft would stop with a jolt when its wheels hit the water, possibly cartwheeling over the nose or a wing. But he noted the wind direction and started the descent, maintaining just enough power for control, while yelling back to Stevens, "Hang on! We're going to hit pretty hard and may nose over. Grab your camera equipment."

Stevens barely had time to prepare himself when the wheels hit the water, and the DH-4B slammed to a stop with no rollout. The abrupt halt flipped the biplane up and over on its back, where it settled down in the soggy, water-soaked sand. For a moment all was quiet. Then, Stevens asked anxiously, "Mac? Are you okay?"

"Yep, at least I think so, haven't moved around much yet," Mac answered.

Slowly and carefully Mac and Stevens crawled out from under the aircraft. They stood up and tried moving their arms and legs to see if everything was in working order. They were fine, but the stalwart plane was a wreck. The wings were torn off; the fuselage was ripped down the side; and the wheel struts were bent. The DeHavilland had to be loaded on an open-end boxcar and shipped to McCook for repairs; the aviators followed by train a few days later.

The first photographic expedition had ended. But nearly two years later, Mac and Stevens would start out on another aerial photographic survey of America.

Back at McCook Field, on June 24, 1924, Mac had dinner with Nelliejay before heading out for the night airways run. She had always liked to fly and tried to find ways into the cockpit whenever an opportunity arose. "Jack," she said to him that night, "won't you take me along on this flight, *please*? I've never been flying at night, and I've been home with the baby for six weeks straight now."

She waited patiently while Mac considered her request.

"I'm sorry, honey, I just can't. We still have slip-ups on these flights at times, and I just don't think it's wise yet. But I will sometime, I promise."

Mac returned to McCook at 8:30 p.m. and checked with the mechanics to be sure that the plane was in tiptop shape. Strapping on his parachute, he climbed into the DeHavilland DH-4B3, and, leaning over the cockpit, felt for the parachute flares. They were in place. So he started the engine, turned on the landing lights, and took off into the darkness.

As McCook's flashing beacon grew dimmer, Mac headed east toward Columbus. He peered ahead through the whirling propeller for the first signs of the next beacon. These revolving lights, situated at Dayton, London, and Columbus, served pilots as guideposts through the dark Ohio sky.

The engine's constant throb helped to keep Mac awake, though the darkness surrounding him tempted him to sleep. Out in the distance, he caught a glimpse of the flickering London beacon that grew stronger as he approached. The lights of Springfield appeared on his left, indicating that he was on course, and soon he was flying over London. When the London beacon disappeared behind him, the Columbus beacon came into view. At Columbus, Mac set the biplane down briefly in the pasture used as a landing spot, pulling the nose up when the wheels had barely skimmed the scrub brush and grass. Then, with half his journey complete, he headed back toward Dayton.

Mac knew that a determined lieutenant named Donald L. Bruner had been responsible for establishing the beacons that were guiding him through the night, and, in the loneliness of his cockpit, Mac silently thanked him.

After World War I, interest in night flying had diminished to almost zero. Arguing that only ten hours of sunlight were available for flying and that seven percent of all flights were canceled because of unfavorable weather, Bruner convinced the Air Service that flying time had to be extended past daylight hours if aviation were ever to become a commercial success. Whether because of his eloquence or his persistence, the Air Service finally gave him permission to start work on proper lighting equipment for planes and landing fields.

Bruner began by developing a reliable landing light that could be carried on an airplane, giving the pilot a clear view of the ground while eliminating the fire dangers posed by the old wing-tip flares. After many experiments, he invented a 300,000-candlepower light that operated on standard 12-volt current and could be mounted on the leading edge of each lower wing to illuminate the ground from 800 feet in the air.

Unfortunately, the new light caused a problem. A pilot who had just made a bad night landing explained: "I got down to the lights and the landing would have been fine, but the glare from the lights through the prop whirling was blinding, and I couldn't see to land."

After new tests and experiments, Bruner determined that a dark maroon color reflected light with the least intensity and promptly had the Air Service repaint all of its propellers.

At McCook Field, Bruner and his team of engineers developed navigational lights encased in red, green, and transparent pyroxylin and mounted on the plane, so they could be seen from all angles of approach.

Most of the ground lights used to illuminate runways blinded pilots and obscured their view of the airfields. During the war, magnesium flares mounted under each of the lower wings could be burned in case of a forced landing in the dark. When ignited, these flares were meant to light the country below, but often they set fire to the wings and destroyed the plane.

Another type of flare was attached to the end of a parachute meant to slow its descent. The Air Service warned pilots not to drop these flares near ammunition depots or dried grass. However, if the sky was dark enough to require flares, the aviators couldn't see what was below. Also, the release mechanism sometimes failed, and, instead of dropping, the flares set fire to the plane and its pilot.

To solve these problems, Bruner came up with the airways flare. Mounted inside the fuselage, the container dropped when the pilot pulled a release handle and ignited when its small parachute was opened. The flare burned for three-and-one-half minutes, descending about 800 feet while aflame.

The new propeller finish, parachute flares, and landing and navigational lights allowed pilots to begin making regular night runs between McCook Field in Dayton and Norton Field in Columbus, a distance of 73 miles.

Commencing on July 3, 1923, this route was flown by test pilots for six weeks every night, and pronounced entirely practical for regular operations. In August of that year, the first trial night Air Mail flights were made successfully between Chicago and Cheyenne, Wyoming, a distance of 885 miles. On July 1, 1924, the first transcontinental night air route began operation between New York and San Francisco.

On Mac's return trip from Columbus the 24th of June, the London beacon once again appeared and receded, and soon after, McCook's beacon flickered in the sky adjacent to the welcoming glow of Dayton. As he approached the outskirts of the city, he glanced at his watch. The time was 10:15 p.m. He had flown 146 miles without any signs of trouble.

Then the engine sputtered and quit.

Mac guessed that the plane was out of gas. Losing precious time as he fumbled blindly for the valve, he switched on the auxiliary fuel tank. Nothing happened. "Maybe I turned it the wrong way," he thought. But after wasting more time trying to locate his flashlight, he discovered that he had turned the valve correctly. He did some quick calculations in his head and decided that McCook Field was close enough to reach in a glide.

Turning the plane to the right in a shallow bank, Mac aimed directly for McCook's beacon. But he quickly realized that his calculations were wrong. He wouldn't be able to reach the air strip.

Mac glided over the center of Dayton where he could see automobile lights traveling the busy streets below. Worried about crashing in such a heavily populated area, he turned the plane toward the largest unlit expanse he could find — the Dayton Community Country Club. If he could make it to the golf course, he could avoid injuring anyone other than himself.

Straining his eyes, Mac noticed that his propeller had stopped revolving. "Now that shouldn't happen just because the engine quit," he said to himself. The air currents should have been enough to keep it rotating. If the original problem had been caused by the failure of the pump or gasoline supply, the engine could only start again when the mechanism turned over and provided a spark. "Maybe that's the trouble. I'll see if I can get the prop rotating with a dive."

Because he had been flying at 5,000 feet — a relatively high altitude — Mac guessed that he had plenty of room to drop. He shoved the stick forward, pointing the nose of the plane toward the ground. As he plunged with the wind shrieking in his ears, he suddenly realized that he was racing toward disaster. The city was directly below.

"What a fool you are, Macready," he berated himself, pulling back the stick as hard as he could. The plane responded slowly, but eventually lifted its nose and entered a shallow glide. With an airspeed of 70 mph, Mac guessed that he might have enough altitude to reach the country club and decided to drop his first flare to illuminate the golf course.

When the lights below had thinned, Mac pulled the first flare handle; nothing happened. So he tried the second flare; but, again, no light appeared under the plane. "Pluto's nether regions couldn't get any darker than this," he thought, as he thrust his head out of the cockpit to see what the trouble was. But all he could see was the dark.

Hills and Dales was an uninhabited section of Dayton that, true to its name, was rough, hilly, and heavily forested. Mac worried that he was headed straight for it instead of the country club. Because Hills and Dales would be a terrible place to make a blind landing, he decided to glide the plane toward another dark spot that he hoped marked the site of the country club and to jump when he reached 1,000 feet. With this in mind, he unbuckled his safety belt, stood up to make sure he was unencumbered, and tested to see if he could control the airplane with his feet.

With the night air blowing straight into his face, visions of "Joe Stiff" raced through Mac's mind.

When Mac's altimeter indicated that he'd reached 1,100 feet, he decided the time had come to bail out. Lifting one leg over the side, he prepared to evacuate, only to find that his parachute had caught on something. With the DH-4B3 plummeting at an alarming rate, he returned to his sitting position, released his hold on the stick, lifted his parachute clear, and climbed over the side once again. As he clung to the wing struts and prepared to jump, the biplane plunged straight down in an irretrievable diving spin.

Mac had practiced this type of emergency many times while lying awake in bed. "Got to be careful. Don't want to make a wrong move. Position my feet right — mustn't get tangled in the wires. . . ." Clutching the wing struts with one hand, he felt for the parachute's release ring with the other. "Got to count two seconds after I jump, then pull the ring," Mac told himself. Then, he let go of the wires and jumped into the Stygian darkness below.

A blurred rush of wings, wood, and engine whipped past him as he tumbled through the powerful slipstream. The city lights appeared above, and then below, while he somersaulted through the air and counted to two. Mac pulled the ring — nothing happened. Images of Joe Stiff's "spilled guts" flashed through his mind. Desperate to avoid Joe's fate, he yanked at the ring again and this time felt a sharp jolt on his shoulders that snapped him upright. The parachute had opened. "Thank God," he thought. But his relief was interrupted by a deafening explosion that ripped through the night. His plane had hit the ground, shooting spectacular flames 50 feet above the horizon.

Then the night fell silent.

Mac could sense the earth rising quickly from below.

"Hello! Hello! Help! Help!" he shouted, hoping someone might hear. "Help, Hello down there. Anyone down there?"

After what seemed to him like an eternity, a tremulous voice called out to him.

"Where are you?"

"Up here in a parachute," Mac answered, just as he crashed into the trees below, grabbing and breaking off branches as he fell. When some branches caught his 'chute, the force swung him into the wall of a deep gorge and then left him dangling 100 feet above the ravine's floor.

Two men came crashing through the brush. "Where are you?" they called out again.

"Over here on the edge of the cliff. I'm stuck."

They all shouted at once. "We're coming. Hold on. Are you hurt?"

"I don't think so," Mac answered, somewhat cautiously.

At the same time that Mac was having trouble in the skies over Dayton, Ed Wuichet, president of the city's Chamber of Commerce, was hosting a dinner party at his country club estate. The guests had enjoyed an extended cocktail hour, imbibed wine with dinner, and adjourned to the terrace for cordials. They were discussing the Bible, most particularly the Book of Revelations and the end of the world, when suddenly, Wuichet cried, "Look at that meteor!" Electrified by the sight of the bright light descending from the sky, the guests jumped to their feet and watched as it slowly sank over the horizon.

The light was one of Mac's flares, which had finally ignited as it fell to earth.

As soon as Wuichet and his guests had returned to their seats, the sound of a terrible crash and, seconds later, the sight of a fiery explosion sent them back to their feet. If the mysterious meteor and the powerful eruption of fire had surprised them, the sepulchral voice they heard shouting, "Help!" froze them in fear.

Wuichet later said that though he was an avid student of the Bible, he had never believed in the Book of Revelations until that night. At the moment, when Mac and his plane fell from the sky, Wuichet felt that Judgment Day had arrived and that the archangel Gabriel was calling down from heaven. He and his terrified guests believed they were witnessing the end of the world!

Mac's two rescuers pulled him from the ravine and took him to the Wuichet home, where he called Nelliejay and the guard at McCook to let them know that he had sustained only minor cuts and bruises. Then one of Wuichet's dinner guests, C. E. Ainsworth, drove him to the wreckage. News of the accident had spread, and the normally deserted roads around the country club were clogged with traffic heading toward the eerie red glow.

The DH-4B3 was still burning when they arrived at the scene of the crash. Because the ravine lay only a few hundred yards from the well-traveled Lebanon Pike Highway, Mac was worried that someone had been injured. He felt relieved to discover that the only thing the biplane had hit was an empty wheat field.

But grief-stricken spectators had gathered around the wreckage and were whispering among themselves that the pilot — one of Dayton's favorite sons — had been cremated in the accident. To end the confusion, Mac pushed his way through the crowd to the light of the burning aircraft while Ainsworth announced, "There's no one in that plane. Lieutenant Macready here jumped out in his parachute!"

Mac reported for duty the next morning, despite his commanding officer's advice to spend the day in bed, with a new appreciation for his friend "Joe Stiff" and that new "contraption." Because his life had been saved by a silk parachute, he became the second member — after Harris — of the Caterpillar Club.

Mac and Stevens, not about to give up the second photographic survey, sent a request to General Patrick. He received it enthusiastically, yet, citing the Air Service's lack of funds, regretfully declined to authorize the expedition. During the 1920s, the Air Service was sometimes so woefully short of money that it couldn't pay its pilots' salaries.

Undaunted, Mac flew to Washington and met with Stevens to find alternative funding. If one department didn't have money, perhaps another would.

Mac and Stevens presented the outline of their project to Stephen Mather, director of the Public Park Service, concluding their pitch with the statement that they were looking for a "good sport" to finance their expedition. Although the Public Park Service had no money, Mather himself did.

"What does it take to qualify as a 'good sport'?" he asked. "I'll put up six dollars a day for sixty days."

Mac and Stevens immediately declared him a *genuine* "good sport." Mathers advanced the funds to the aviators, giving them blanket authority to determine their itinerary and subjects.

The Air Service, in its magnanimity, put an Army DeHavilland at their disposal, yet failed to include the fuel. The two airmen accepted the offer anyway and took off on July 18, 1925, almost two years after their first photo expedition.

Advance publicity about the flight brought letters from various Chambers of Commerce throughout the United States, inviting Mac and Stevens to stop at their towns and accept their hospitality. Free hospitality tempted the two fliers to put these spots on their route; for three dollars per day, each, hardly covered the cost of food, lodging, and gasoline. Nevertheless, Mac and Stevens resisted many offers. If an invitation came from a town that happened to be near their destination, Mac requested information regarding the condition of the field (if the town had one), its dimensions, and a list of any obstructions such as fences, trees, buildings, or high mountains. He also asked for the direction of the prevailing winds.

Mac described the parameters the DeHavilland needed to land:

> We must be careful of such things as stumps, badger holes, or
> other obstructions lying on the field, and a normal landing field
> for an airplane such as we will be flying should be at least 1,800
> to 2,000 feet long and should have a smooth, level surface.

They found few such fields.

Armed with camera, film, maps, a change of underwear, a few dollars, and a lot of courage and determination, the two intrepid airmen set out for the eight-week odyssey. Stevens shot 2,000 aerial photographs during the journey.

Mac and Stevens had no parachutes nor brakes on their plane; they had no first-aid kits and no food on board. Most of their stopovers were one-night stands, but in several areas, such as Montana, they established a base headquarters and made daily sorties to photograph points of interest within range. Their expedition covered all 48 states and 10,000 miles.

Making day trips from Kalispell, Montana, Mac and Stevens took the first aerial photographs of Glacier National Park. Lewis' Glacier Park Hotel, on the west side of Lake McDonald, had been a fur-trading site for Meriwether Lewis, in the early 1800s, and the local tribes. At the time of Mac's and Stevens's visit, the area was still rather remote, and the local Indians greeted them cautiously. Stevens, who wanted to photograph some of them, wasn't discouraged by their unfriendliness. Solemnly and ceremoniously, he brought Mac to the chief and formally introduced him as "chief of the flying section, McCook Field." Mac, right on cue, introduced Stevens as "chief of the photographic branch, McCook Field." Confronted by two illustrious "chiefs," the Indian chief graciously consented to pose for the camera and organized a war dance and concert. Stevens had a day of extraordinary opportunity snapping pictures.

Later, Mac described this part of the trip:

> There was some fine scenery in Glacier Park, different than other territory over which we had flown. We flew at various altitudes. One of the peculiar formations we saw was so regular in shape one could hardly believe it was not the work of man. From the sky it looked like pyramids. Park men told us we had probably flown over territory that no living person had seen before. We took pictures from the Canadian line to the south end of the park.

During this trip, Mac and Stevens photographed the Rocky Mountain National Park, Pikes Peak, Holy Cross, and most of Colorado; the Great Salt Lake, the Wasatch Mountains, and Reno, Carson City, Virginia City, and the Comstock Lode in Nevada; the old gold workings of California, Lake Tahoe, Yosemite, Mount Tamalpais, the Salmon Alps, Mount Shasta, Death Valley, Mount Whitney, and Sequoia National Park in California; Mount Hood and the Columbia River in Oregon and Washington; Mount Rainier, the Olympic Mountains in Washington; Glacier National Park, Montana; Jackson Hole, Yellowstone National Park, the Grand Canyon of the Yellowstone in Wyoming; the Sawtooth Mountains of Idaho; Bryce

Canyon, Cedar Breaks, and Zion National Park in Utah; Mount Charleston, Kings River Canyon, and Boulder Canyon, the Northern Rim of the Grand Canyon, in Nevada; the Painted Desert, the Petrified Forest, and Meteor Crater in Arizona; as well as cities, universities, and landing fields.

Because so many of the towns they flew into were off the beaten path of fliers, Mac and Stevens serviced the plane themselves. Each day, after many hours in the air and taking photographs and when the gas supply ran low, they would head toward the nearest flat pasture or field. Flying close to the ground, Mac would "drag" the area for possible ditches, logs, gullies, fences, jackrabbit and badger holes, or other obstructions that might ruin their landing and their day. Swirling dust, rippling water, and tossing trees indicated which way the wind was blowing. When he had found a safe landing area, he pushed the nose of the biplane forward for the descent, circled the chosen spot, and landed.

Throughout this low-level maneuvering the townspeople would hurry toward them on foot, horseback, or car, for many had never seen an airplane before. After landing, Mac taxied to the most desirable looking corner of the field, where he and Stevens could climb out, introduce themselves to the curious spectators, explain their mission, and inquire about the availability of high octane gasoline — a rhetorical question in most areas. Usually the only available gas was an inferior grade, which increased the danger of engine sputtering or misfiring.

But in most areas, big drums of fuel would arrive on the back of trucks. For approximately an hour and a half, men would empty 143 gallons of gasoline into the plane by lifting it up in five-gallon pails to someone standing on top of the engine, who then poured it into the gas tank through a funnel covered with a chamois to strain out any impurities.

The airmen drove stakes into the ground and tied the plane down securely, but Mac always arranged for a guard to stay overnight with the plane; he never left cameras, film equipment, or baggage inside, for experience had proven that these items disappeared too easily. The pilots covered the engine and cockpits with canvas, checked the tires, and made any necessary repairs or adjustments before leaving the plane for the night — and then, Stevens took his run.

Mac explained later that he would never forget the first time he was initiated into Steven's exercise program. They had flown all day, landing toward late afternoon near a small Western town in Montana called Big Timber. After the two men had gassed the plane and had almost finished some minor repair work on the engine, Stevens turned to Mac and asked, "Mac, think you can finish this up alone? I'd like to get my run in."

"Sure, go ahead," Mac replied, not knowing exactly what he meant.

Stevens disappeared into the rear cockpit for a few minutes. A crowd of about 40 people stood around the aircraft, waiting for the men to finish their work so that they could escort them into town and put them up for the night. When Stevens emerged from the cockpit, the onlookers gasped, for he was dressed in a "regulation" track suit. Leaping nimbly over the side of the biplane, he started off across the sagebrush-covered prairie with the long regular strides of a trained runner and soon disappeared from view.

After his initial surprise, Mac returned to his work on the engine as though nothing unusual had happened. About 20 minutes later, as he finished his repairs, a white speck appeared on the horizon, growing larger as it neared, until he could make out Stevens running toward him. Reaching the plane, Stevens climbed back into the cockpit without comment and emerged minutes later in his uniform.

Stevens' "track suit" consisted of nothing more than his regular underwear with narrow bands of red silk sewn along the sides. He claimed that if a man took off his clothes and ran around in his briefs, he would be arrested. But if he had small red ribbons sewn around his waist, down the sides, and around the legs of these same garments, he felt perfectly presentable. He was right, for he never had any trouble over his "running suit."

. . . It is requested that Lieutenants James H. Doolittle and John A. Macready be permitted to make this flight. . . . Both pilots have over 1700 hours in the air and are familiar with cross-country work and the preparation necessary for the successful accomplishment of long flights.

Chapter 10

One More River to Cross — The TransPacific Flight

OR JOHN MACREADY, as for all the test pilots at Dayton's McCook Field, a single accomplishment or world record was never enough. Somewhere out there lay another challenge, some other unknown waiting to be explored. He thrived on conquering that which seemed impossible. Yet, simply deciding to fly where no one had flown before was the easy part; every new pursuit required hours of research and, most importantly, official approval.

Some seven months after the May 2 coast-to-coast flight, in December 1923, Mac sent his plans for a transPacific flight — along with a warning about possible competition from the Navy — to Jimmy Doolittle, his friend at the Massachusetts Institute of Technology. (Doolittle later gained fame during World War II leading the B-25 bombing attack on Tokyo.)

> Just before Commander Smith left McCook Field, it came out on the front page of the Dayton newspapers to the effect that the Navy intended to make the transPacific flight and had the whole project doped out identically with our own. It looks to me as if he put two and two together and obtained the idea and his data through our talks and your study about navigation under him. This is old Navy stuff and inasmuch as they are really the logical ones, from the standpoint of equipment, to put it over, we may have considerable trouble.

Two years earlier, in 1921, General Billy Mitchell had demonstrated the superiority of airpower by sinking three German battleships captured during World War I. The *Ostfriesland*, considered unsinkable by seapower strategists, went down in less than 22 minutes after bombs dropped from Air Service planes smashed in her hull and blew holes in her deck. Since then, the Navy had eagerly challenged the Army's aviation superiority. Although the rivalry was mostly friendly, neither branch ever missed an opportunity to upstage or outdo the other. This attitude prevailed from the lowest-ranking privates and seamen to the highest-ranking generals and admirals.

As the only naval officer at McCook Field, John Price received much good-natured ribbing from the Air Service test pilots. In an effort to uphold the Navy's tradition and reputation, he often went overboard demonstrating his prowess as a flier. He was known as something of a "hotshot," a reckless fireball who had a lot of close calls and never missed a chance to show off. But one day he went too far and ended up, much to his chagrin, with the proverbial egg on his face.

As Price approached McCook Field after a routine flight, he couldn't resist buzzing up North Riverdale Street and over the Dayton View section of the city where many of the Air Service test pilots lived. In his enthusiasm, he forgot about his gas supply, and, as he pulled out of the last low buzz, his engine sputtered and died. He swung the nose of the aircraft around, hoping that, with luck, he might be able to nurse the old DeHavilland DH-4B in a shallow glide back to the McCook flying area and that, by landing safely, he might retain his honor and reputation. But Price calculated incorrectly, for as he swung over Sutmillers Nightclub and Restaurant on North Main, barely skimming the rooftops and trees, he hit a telephone guide wire. Without breaking the wire, the plane slid into a telephone pole and terminated its forward progress in the top of a maple tree.

Fred Marshall, the editor of the base newspaper, was walking from the Canoe Club down to his room on Linwood Street, when he spotted Price thrashing around in the tree branches over his head.

"I say, can you get me a rope or ladder or something?" Price called.

"Are you sure you're all right?" Marshall replied. "Are you hurt?"

"Oh sure, I'm all right. I just need a little help getting down from here. But as for that old crate," the "Navy man" said, gesturing disdainfully toward the biplane, "it's a good thing it's going to the junkyard before some of those schoolboy Army pilots over at the field kill themselves in it."

In January 1924, Mac approached Major McIntosh, McCook Field's chief of the engineering division, about the transPacific flight. They talked for over an hour, then climbed into McIntosh's car and drove down to inspect the Fokker Ambulance T-2, sister ship of the Fokker T-2 Transport that Mac and Kelly had flown across the country. From there, they visited the radio laboratory to see how the direction-finding equipment worked.

"The best way to handle this is to go right down to Washington and see General Patrick about it. Tell him what you have in mind and give him the whole picture," McIntosh told Mac. "The General will be back in Washington after the seventeenth of this month, and you could fly down after that."

But by January 17, Mac was too busy with the supercharger high-altitude tests to leave McCook. So he wrote another letter to Doolittle:

> If I can't get to Washington, I'll send you all the dope I've worked up on the flight so you can talk to the general intelligently when he comes to Boston on the twenty-eighth.

Because of Mac's previous success with the Fokker T-2 monoplane, he wanted to use it for the transPacific flight. But, as he mentioned to Doolittle in a February letter: "The T-2 is now in the Smithsonian Institute in Washington, and we may have some trouble getting it out again."

When Mac mentioned to McIntosh his desire to use the T-2, the Major also had doubts about the possibility of extricating the aircraft from its resting place in the Smithsonian.

"I think you'd have a great deal of difficulty in getting General Patrick to go through all the red tape necessary to have the T-2 taken out again," he replied. "Why don't you look into the possibility of using the Douglas World Cruiser or remodeling the ambulance T-2 here at McCook."

Upon General Patrick's February visit to M.I.T., Doolittle asked him if Mac and he could speak with him in March about the transPacific flight.

"Yes. I'll be back in my office by then," Patrick replied, in a tone indicating that he was less than eager to pursue the subject. Doolittle didn't press the General because he was busy. Doolittle wrote Mac that same day:

> I am not particularly disappointed over my failure to get an interview with him here, as the time and atmosphere did not seem propitious. If you can come to Washington with me, I believe it would greatly strengthen our chances. Believe, however, I planted a small seed and recalled to his mind your conversation with him of some time past. It is possible that in turning it over in his mind, he may be favorably impressed and in a more receptive mood a couple of weeks hence.

Unable to get away from his duties at McCook Field, Mac finally gave up on the idea of a personal appeal and sent an official memorandum to General Patrick's headquarters in Washington, requesting permission to make the trip, and signed both his and Doolittle's names. The request was dated March 12, 1924, and contained the following outline:

```
Route From San Francisco to Honolulu  . . . . .2395 miles
From Honolulu to Island of Midway  . . . . . . .1325 miles
From Island of Midway to Island of Wake  . . .1200 miles
From Island of Wake to Island of Guam . . . . .1515 miles
From Island of Guam to Manila . . . . . . . . . .1640 miles
From Manila to Hong Kong.  . . . . . . . . . . . . .685 miles
       Total: . . . . . . . . . . . . . . . . . . . . . . . . .8760 miles
```

It is requested that Lieutenants James H. Doolittle and John A. Macready be permitted to make this flight. Both are graduates of the A.S. [Air Service] Engineering School and are familiar with the testing, construction, maintenance and upkeep of airplanes. . . . Both pilots have over 1700 hours in the air and are familiar with cross-country work and the preparation necessary for the successful accomplishment of long flights. Lieutenant Doolittle is familiar with navigation. Lieutenant Macready completed over 20,000 miles of cross-country flying last year.

The memorandum offered the general details on navigation:

Two types of navigation would be used: direction finding by means of radio and the terrestrial navigation used on the sea. The primary method would be by means of radio direction finding. Satisfactory radio towers are now in existence at San Diego, Honolulu, Guam, and Manila. The Island of Wake is uninhabited. Midway is a cable station and almost uninhabited. It would be necessary to build 5 K.W. [kilowatt] stations from the ground up, including the primary source of power on Wake and Midway. By making use of material already existing, the total cost of equipment to guide a plane accurately and safely from San Diego to the Philippines by way of Hawaii, Midway, Wake and Guam, would not exceed $6000. The earth inductor compass, which can be installed for [*a total weight of*] eight pounds, will be used to supplement the ordinary compass on this trip. This will not only facilitate navigation, but will be the best practical test which can be devised for this new instrument.

Mac also discussed night flying, which was still in the experimental stage:

One night flight would be required since, by taking advantage of an early start, all legs of the flight, with the exception of the one between San Francisco and Honolulu, could be made without darkness.

Because of his troubles with the mountain ranges on the transcontinental flight, Mac added a paragraph on elevations:

> Although the navigation would probably be more difficult, the flight as a whole should be simpler and easier than the transcontinental flight, from the actual flying, engine, and airplane standpoint, as there would be no elevations to contend with. The engine could be throttled for practically the entire distance.

In case General Patrick thought this project was too ambitious, Mac explained:

> Should the time for preparation appear too short to permit accomplishment of this project by next May, or the chief of Air Service not see fit to authorize this flight at that time, it is requested that the above named pilots be permitted to make a non-stop flight from San Francisco to Honolulu.

Navigation on this island-hopping flight would be their biggest problem, so Mac's memorandum described the crew's need for an expert navigator to relieve the pilots of the bulk of the navigational work. Although Doolittle was then studying navigation, Mac felt he could justify Lieutenant Bradley Jones' extra 160 pounds, for Jones was a reserve officer and navigator with practical experience and knowledge of Pacific Ocean conditions, having been a ship's navigator for many years in the region. By eliminating 28 gallons of gasoline, the plane's total weight would remain the same.

Two weeks later, General Patrick sent word that he would visit McCook Field, causing Mac to speculate that he had looked favorably on the request and was coming to discuss it more fully. Mac was filled with cautious optimism. Major McIntosh arranged for a conference with the General. But before Patrick arrived on March 25, Mac's official memorandum was returned to McCook with the following rejection:

> Although the chief of Air Service appreciates the spirit which

prompts a request of this nature and is confident that Lieutenants Macready and Doolittle are more than qualified to initiate such a project, with every prospect of success, it is not feasible to grant approval for this flight at the present time. At present, all of the resources of the Air Service are concentrated on the successful completion of the round-the-world flight and it is not desirable that any other project of such magnitude be considered prior to its conclusion.

General Patrick disappointed Mac by canceling their conference at McCook. Perhaps he wished to avoid any more persuasion. Yet, Mac hoped that he would have a chance to talk to Patrick when he flew him to St. Louis later in the day. However, the General changed his plans and went by train instead.

Undaunted, Mac wrote to Jimmy Doolittle saying that he was to ferry the General from St. Louis to McCook the following Friday and that he would talk to Patrick then. "It looks, however, as though the chances are slim," he wrote, "although I will put up a hard fight."

General Patrick traveled by train as far as Terre Haute, then turned around and went back to Washington. Because Patrick once again had changed his plans, Mac lost another opportunity to plead his case. Major McIntosh advised Mac against making an immediate trip to Washington to attempt reversing the General's decision, so Mac postponed the project for a few months.

Having learned that the Fokker T-2 was permanently unavailable, Mac began to search for another airplane capable of making the transPacific flight. The Loening Amphibian COA, AS (Air Service) 24-8, built by Grover Loening, was one of the aircraft under consideration for the flight, but Mac eventually found the Stout Air Pullman, a six-passenger high-wing airliner. The American-built Stout's design, was similar to the T-2, and also was powered by a single Liberty-12 engine.

In a letter to William B. Stout, Mac outlined the project, setting forth his requirements regarding performance, economy, interior arrangement, and endurance. He also suggested that he was interested in any ideas that would provide safety in an unexpected ocean landing. Because of competition from the Navy, he asked Stout to "kindly consider this confidential." Mac concluded with some subtle persuasion: "It would be desirable to use the Stout if you are interested in having an airplane bearing your name undertake a venture as outlined in the attachment."

William Stout liked the idea of having his name and his aircraft used for such an ambitious adventure.

⟨∿⟩

Mac flew to Washington during the first week in May 1924. When he dropped by Patrick's office, the General was absent, so he discussed the flight with Major Frank, the executive officer. "If you put through your request next year when the around-the-world flight is completed, you could expect a favorable reply," Frank suggested.

Since the successful flights of the Wright Brothers, aviators from many countries had hoped to be the first to fly all the way around the world. After World War I, when British, French, Italian, Portuguese, and Argentine airmen began planning to attempt such a flight, General Patrick announced America's intention of entering the contest. But unlike the Europeans and South Americans, the U.S. Air Service would fly their Douglas World Cruisers westward. The large biplanes, powered by single 420-hp Liberty-12 engines, were modified from the military Douglas DT-2 and equipped with wheels and pontoons. Extra gasoline and oil tanks had been added to increase range of flight.

On April 6, 1924, a team of seven pilots had relayed from Seattle to Sitka, Prince Rupert, Ketchikan, Cordova, Yukutat Bay, Chignik, Japan, Hong Kong, Siam, Burma, Calcutta, Karachi, Bagdad, Paris, London, Reykjavik, Greenland, and back to Boston. Five World Cruisers began the attempt; one crashed in Alaska and one sank at sea north of Scotland. The remaining three returned to Seattle September 28, 1924.

Despite the successful completion of the around-the-world-flight, Mac and Doolittle never received support for their transPacific flight.

⟨∿⟩

Over a year later, in late fall of 1925, Sir Hubert Wilkins, the Detroit Aviation Society, and their financial backers asked Mac and Doolittle to fly an expedition over the North Pole. In December, the two aviators flew to Detroit for four days of conferences on details of the trip with Wilkins, H. G. McCarroll, Vilhjalmur Stefansson, and representatives of the Ford Motor Company.

At first, the hazards of a 2,500-mile flight over a frozen sea of rugged moving ice tempered the fliers' enthusiasm. Their course would take them over terrain where the white mist hanging over the ice blends with the general monotony to obscure the horizon; where the sun's low position ruins the light and visibility; where the use of navigational instruments is difficult because of this lack of sunlight; and where the compass performs erratically in reaction to the magnetic pole. The prospect of walking a thousand miles across the ice in minus 30 degree temperatures — if forced to land — wasn't appealing. But as Wilkins provided Mac and Doolittle with more information about Arctic conditions and their preparations progressed, they grew more enthusiastic about making the trip.

During these discussions, Mac met several wealthy and influential men who, in his words, "were extremely good sports." He used the opportunity to pitch another of his pet projects — a photographic expedition to Mount Everest — to a Mr. Evans and Mr. George T. Bye, of George Palmer Putnam, Inc., who expressed interest in backing the project.

As Mac and Doolittle returned to McCook, Mac, who was piloting their DeHavilland, encountered a blinding snowstorm, which cut visibility to nearly zero and gave them a preview of conditions in the Arctic. Although a skilled pilot, Mac had a bit of trouble locating the city of Dayton through the blizzard. Eventually, he spotted the field and landed safely.

❧

General Patrick, who was visiting McCook, happened to be in Mac's office when one of the polar expedition backers telephoned. After Mac's lengthy conversation, the General asked for details about this proposed flight, which Mac gladly provided. He also told Patrick that he and Doolittle wanted very much to make the trip. Patrick listened carefully, said that he would study the matter, then walked out.

Shortly after this conversation, Mac received a telegram from Mr. McCarroll: "Please wire me immediately at Mayflower Hotel, Washington, list of major items of necessary equipment."

Mac wired McCarroll, requesting two Douglas C-1 Transport biplanes, equipped with single 420-hp Liberty-12 engines carrying large gasoline tanks and all the necessary spare parts for a transpolar flight. He asked for radio equipment, an expert weather forecaster, two expert mechanics, and a complete set of polar-region maps.

A week later, after McCarroll had returned to Detroit from his discussions with General Patrick in Washington, he wrote Mac thanking him for his comprehensive telegram, adding:

> As matters now stand, we are to get two Douglas Transports to be tested and equipped at McCook Field. These planes are to be rented to us at a nominal figure, and to be replaced only in event of a crash.

His next sentence sent Mac into a fit of despair.

> Unfortunately it looks very much as if we shall not be allowed to have the benefit of yours and Lieutenant Doolittle's valuable experience on the expedition. Both General Patrick and Secretary Davis are extremely reluctant to release you men as, confidentially, we were told that you were the two most valuable men the Air Service had.

The decision, McCarroll felt, was such a severe blow to the expedition, that the Detroit Aviation Society gave up the idea of a non-stop flight from Point Barrow, Alaska, to Spitzbergen, Norway, and, instead, conducted exploration work of the Arctic with a three-engine Fokker plane.

Mac was crushed.

But Mac had other plans. Along with his good friend Captain A. W. Stevens, Mac had wished to make a photographic survey of Mount Everest, in the Himalayas. Stevens believed that aerial photographs would map the area's topography for the benefit of scientific societies, some of whom had already expressed a willingness to underwrite the expedition. The total cost would be about $100,000, with the Air Service providing the airplane equipment and the regular monthly wages of the two officers.

Mac liked this project and pushed for the building of a high-altitude photographic airplane, officially requesting that a set of wings, like those that had been especially designed for high-altitude flight, be built for the XCO-5 airplane No. P-305. This biplane, which had been adapted for supercharger installation, could climb to 33,000 feet, making it an ideal photographic platform. Mac wrote that

> photographs of the ground from altitudes above 30,000 feet would be possible through its use, and would be of great military value. A vertical photo from this altitude might provide a map of sufficient size to include both lines of attack. Distances and angles of fire could be estimated, and the airplane itself could not be seen from the ground.

He recommended the following program to General Billy Mitchell:

1) that the airplane be flight tested and used to break the world altitude record;
2) that Mount Everest be photographed and mapped from above;
3) that Mount McKinley and the inaccessible country of Alaska be photographed and mapped;
4) that high-altitude scenic oblique pictures be taken of areas such as the Great Lakes, New York City and its harbor, and other regions of general interest.

Although General Mitchell authorized Mac to proceed with the modifications to the new XCO-5 high-altitude aircraft, the Mount Everest survey never progressed beyond the planning stage.

During the early 1920s, the test pilots and engineers at McCook Field helped to transform aviation from a nascent mode of transportation, which had primarily been the domain of hobbyists and inventors, into a viable commercial and military industry. And with such development, their imagination, their ingenuity, and their will eventually ran into the ubiquitous barriers of bureaucracy and financing. Nevertheless, their numerous accomplishments compensated for their inevitable frustrations.

. . . The 1920s are considered to be the first quantum advancement in aeronautical technology. . . . the first non-stop flight across the United States, the first night-airways run, the first parachute jumps, the first crop-dusting from the air, the first aerial photographic survey of America . . . the first probing flights into space. . . .

Chapter 11

The End of an Era —
The Final Years
at McCook Field

N LATE 1925, Mac prepared to break another world altitude record. Accordingly, the engineering section at McCook Field prepared the specially built supercharged XCO-5 biplane for him. *The New York Times*, which had been following the high-altitude tests, described the plane's wings as follows:

The type selected to give the high lift desired was the Joukowsky StAe-27-A, a set of which was built in the engineering shops. Of wood and fabric construction, they are heavily cambered, having an extremely thick chord at the leading edge and tapering sharply to the rear. Gap and stagger are pronounced. A detachable blade aluminum alloy propeller ten feet six inches in length, with pitch being adjustable on the ground, was installed on the plane.

On December 15, 1925, Mac sent a formal request to his superiors for authorization to attempt the flight and received the following reply: "Permission granted." Once again, he would challenge France — perennial aviation rival of the United States — in the skies.

Although Mac wanted to break the world altitude record, he also wanted to test various apparatus in the rarefied atmosphere above 30,000 feet. In any war, the nation having the highest flying aircraft would be the most likely victor; an airplane operating at an altitude of 40,000 feet would be out of sight of land forces, out of range of anti-aircraft guns, and out of hearing range from the ground. No one knew the ceiling of the XCO-5, and therein lay the possibility of an altitude record. At the time, the record was 39,586 feet, established on October 10, 1924, by the Frenchman M. Callizo.

McCook Field engineers had built a queer-looking oxygen machine that they claimed was as foolproof and as perfect as human ingenuity could make it. Starting at 25,000 feet, Mac would depend on this contraption for his oxygen supply. He would don his usual two suits of woolen underwear, his regular uniform, and a heavily padded flying suit of feathers quilted between silk and lined on the outside by leather. His fleece-lined moccasins went on over several pairs of wool socks. Fur-lined gloves, the oxygen mask, and gelatin-covered goggles completed his "space" suit. Movement, needless to say, was stiff and awkward.

Newspaper reports generated national interest in the flight. Mac received bundles of mail from well-wishers, prophets of gloom and doom, and people with well-meaning suggestions. Among the latter, Vilhjalmur Stefansson from New York, offered Mac the benefit of his experience on an Arctic expedition:

On that trip we wore clothing made entirely of caribou skin and mountain sheepskin, cut on the Eskimo pattern, with two hooded shirts, one worn with the fur next to the body and the other worn with the fur outside. Clothing of this kind will keep a fellow warm in the coldest blizzard that ever blew.

But Mac had already tested such suits and determined that they were insufficient protection for high-altitude work.

Subjecting his body to the intense strain of high-altitude flying required Mac to keep in top physical shape. Lester Maitland, one of the test pilots at McCook and the author of *Knights of the Air*, described Mac as

> a man of many professions. He can qualify as a miner, rancher, boxer, lawyer, and justice of the peace. He is good-natured, rather silent, and a remarkable non-stop listener. His hobby is athletics. He was once amateur light-weight boxing champion of the Pacific Coast, and he still keeps himself in splendid physical trim. It is probably due to the extreme care with which Macready treats himself that he has succeeded in establishing his various altitude records. Macready and his ships are always in perfect condition.

On January 29, 1926, a bitterly cold, windy winter day, the XCO-5 biplane awaited its pilot on the frost-covered ground. Once again, as they had done years earlier on Mac's endurance flight, Orville Wright and officials from the *Fédération Aéronautique Internationale* stood along the flight line to confirm that the instruments were properly loaded. Mac climbed in and taxied out for an official attempt at the current altitude record.

With an engine sluggish from the cold, Mac took off from McCook Field in the early dawn hours and returned within an hour. Although the XCO-5 had performed flawlessly, the supercharger had failed to function above 25,000 feet, dooming the flight to failure. Nevertheless, Mac had set a new American altitude record and had come within 800 feet of the world record. "Had [the supercharger] functioned properly there is every reason to believe a new world record would have been set," Mac told reporters when he landed.

After a careful examination, the engineers found a large crack in the inter-cooler, which had allowed compressed air to escape. Concerned over press coverage regarding the failure of its product, General Electric, the manufacturer of the supercharger, sent Mac a letter asking him to correct the impression that the supercharger had failed. They asked him to explain before his next flight, that the "supercharger [was] not at fault, but a cracked pipe connecting the supercharger with the engine allowed compressed air to leak out instead of being forced into the carburetor."

Mac responded to GE's request:

> I will do what I can to correct the impression circulated by the press that the supercharger failed in my previous flight. By that I mean that I will try and correct the impression that some part of the supercharger broke. What really did happen was that the air intercooler cracked in two places, and in addition to this I do not think that the supercharger had the capacity which it has had on other attempts for a record. In other words, zero altitude was obtained with this supercharger only to an altitude of 24,500 feet when, with the superchargers which I have used before, I have been able to keep zero altitude to 33,000 feet. *[Without a supercharger, the Liberty-12, which normally developed 400 hp at sea level, would only produce 87 hp at 25,000 feet.]* I try to give a totally unbiased statement on completion of one of these flights that will injure no one, but it is difficult to control the press; in fact, it is impossible.
>
> The only headlines in Dayton papers were "Macready Fails." The supercharger was mentioned in the text, but the impression left was that I had quit for some reason or other and I personally do not like this any more than you like the unwelcome publicity regarding the supercharger. In this particular case, it was the supercharger and intercooler which caused failure. On landing I stated that I had held zero altitude to only 24,500 feet which was practically the only statement which was made by me.

The supercharger continued to frustrate Mac and the engineers. While waiting for the weather to break, Mac made various short-altitude flights to test the supercharger's performance, but reached zero altitude 8,000 to 9,000 feet lower than he had during earlier flights.

On the morning of March 13, 1927, at 9:35 a.m., with Orville Wright and officials of the FAI standing by, Mac climbed into the XCO-5 biplane and took off, only to return shortly because of ignition trouble. At 10:43 a.m., the repairs were complete, and he took off again. With perfect weather and visibility conditions, the aircraft, trailing a white ribbon of exhaust gasses, climbed into the sky and vanished into the stratosphere.

Mac climbed to an indicated altitude of 39,000 feet (a figure which, when calibrated, he felt sure would be a new world's record). After landing 1 hour and 56 minutes later, he claimed, "I believe I reached the absolute limit of the plane."

"Did you make it?" all the observers asked him.

"If the Bureau of Standards does its stuff," he said with a grin.

Although officials, including Orville Wright, initially believed that the instruments indicated a new world altitude record, after completing their calibrations, they announced that no record had been set.

In the 1920s, pay for servicemen was low, so good men often left the service to take more lucrative positions with private companies, which occasionally raided McCook for mechanics, engineers, and test pilots, offering high salaries as an inducement. Harold Harris joined Huff-Daland Dusters, Inc.; Shorty Schroeder took a job with the Ford Motor Company; and Corliss C. Moseley accepted a position as vice-president of Western Air Express in Los Angeles. Yet despite the temptation, most of the McCook Field personnel were more interested in their pioneering aviation work than in money.

Eager to find a way to supplement his low military salary, Mac decided to do some business on the side. In a letter to Colonel Paul Henderson, assistant postmaster general, he outlined his plans:

> In conformance with the most recently established policy of the Post Office Department to purchase future airplanes from actual flying samples, it is intended to submit a sample plane for entry in the mail plane competition originally advertised for March 13, 1925. This airplane is now under construction by Dayton capitalists and manufacturers of integrity, is being built to function as a mail-carrying plane under the conditions existing in the Air Mail Service, is 60 percent finished with jigs, dies, and full production drawings for the entire airplane.
>
> The airplane has fifty-seven cubic feet of mail space, can efficiently carry 1000 pounds of mail, has a high speed of 130

m.p.h., a landing speed of 50 m.p.h., and a high factor of safety.

It will be submitted to the Mail Service for a price of less than $8500 without Liberty engine.

Mac's design called for the framework to be constructed of chrome molybdenum steel tubing. The fuselage covering of a combination of plywood and duralumin was a new idea for the time. Duralumin had a smooth surface for better air flow and weathered better than plywood or fabric. The engines were mounted in tandem over the top of the plane. The Dayton Aircraft Corporation, of which Mac was vice-president, at Wilbur Wright Field, built the first prototype. Studebaker Securities Company, of Chicago, Mac's financial backer for the project, planned to name the plane after Macready and manufacture it for commercial and express transport use.

By June 1, 1925, Mac had his airplane covered, had the wings installed, and had it flown to Cleveland, Ohio, and Monmouth, Illinois, before returning to Dayton.

Although he had withdrawn his airmail plane from Post Office Department competition because construction delays had prevented him from meeting their deadline, he had completed arrangements with Mr. R. G. Weyant, in McKeesport, Pennsylvania, to manufacture the plane. But Fairchild, Ford, and Rickenbacker also expressed interest in his plane and came to Dayton to look it over. He felt certain that only a few engineering tests stood between that day and the actual manufacture and sale of the aircraft.

Unknown to Mac, the engineers had removed two additional inter-plane struts, which were originally installed at each wingtip, during their tests. So when Hoy Barksdale tested the plane on March 24, a bad wing flutter developed, causing the rear and front spars to fail. The left wing raised, then the airplane rolled to the left. Barksdale opened his safety belt and jumped, suffering only minor injuries — a severely sprained ankle, a severely strained muscle, and multiple contusions. The aircraft fared far worse, having been totally destroyed along with the Liberty motor Mac had borrowed from the government. He had no insurance to cover the loss.

By the spring of 1926, the Air Service began phasing out McCook Field. Engineering, procurement, and supply were moved to the new Wright Field, and the aviation section would soon follow.

As a war emergency, McCook had served its purpose. But as the Air Service grew, it found that the rent it was paying for McCook was too high, and the field was too small for experimental work. Surrounded on three sides by the Miami River and the city of Dayton, McCook couldn't grow. Furthermore, it supported 69 wooden buildings that were too expensive to maintain and to heat and that were also fire hazards.

The days of "flying by the seat of your pants," the experimental "cut and try" days, were drawing to a close. Research, the drawing board, and technology would soon take over. The engineering department would remove much of the elements of chance before an aircraft left the ground.

The 1920s are considered to be the first quantum advancement in aeronautical technology. During this decade, the first non-stop flight across the United States, the first night-airways run, the first parachute jumps, the first crop-dusting from the air, the first aerial photographic survey of America — and perhaps most importantly — the first probing flights into space developed more systematic, less personal, approaches to understanding the nature of manned flight.

For Mac, the McCook years had been a period of close personal friendships and cooperation, of pranks and camaraderie, of courage and patriotism, of loyalty and personal grief. He felt the changes deeply. He was 39 years old; he loved the Air Service, but wondered if he should so freely risk his life when he had a young family to support. The pay was terrible, and private industry was knocking at his door.

In January 1926, Mac officially requested a four-month leave of absence at the conclusion of his high-altitude work. His request was denied. In a letter to his old friend Oakley Kelly, Mac wrote:

> As you saw in the paper, I have been ordered to Panama, but the chances are at least ten-to-one that I will resign from the Army at the end of this month as I have been offered an extremely good position with General Motors Corporation.

But, Mac wished to maintain his ties to the Air Service, and so, as several other pilots had done before him, his second request was for one year's leave of absence without pay. In the meantime, General Patrick had decided that no more Air Service officers would be granted a year's leave. However, Mac knew of at least one officer who, having been turned down when he applied through regular channels, had his leave approved through political channels — with the help of the Ford Motor Company. An executive with the National Cash Register Company attempted to help Mac in his endeavor, yet General Patrick still refused to grant Mac's request.

Afterward, Mac always wondered if perhaps an incident several years before had somehow prejudiced Patrick against him. The General had made a well-publicized visit to McCook Field, and when his plane touched down and taxied to a stop on the apron, Mac had been on hand to help him alight. As Patrick, a brusque, ramrod-straight, unsociable type, stepped down and proceeded to take off his helmet, Mac reached over to help him. Inadvertently, Mac pulled off the General's wig along with the helmet. Patrick was speechless with rage at the public revelation of his well-kept secret.

For this or some other reason, Mac never received his leave of absence.

In April 1926, John A. Macready, 39-year-old captain and chief test pilot for the United States Air Service, simultaneous holder of the world's altitude, endurance, and distance records, and the only three-time winner of the Mackay Trophy, left the military for civilian life. He had logged 2,428 total hours of flight time.

The entire base turned out for the banquet in his honor, for he was well-liked and well-respected. In an emotional moment at the conclusion of the banquet, held in the fully packed big hangar at McCook Field, the test pilots of the aviation section presented Mac with a splendid silver military sword encased in an elaborately embossed gold-trimmed sheath, upon which was engraved:

> To Captain John A. Macready, USAS
> From Flying Section, Engineering Division
> McCook Field, April 17, 1926

Holding back tears, Mac accepted the gift from his fellow aviators, and his voice broke occasionally as he said his good-byes:

It is lonely work fighting the elements at the earth's ceiling, but I hope that my six years spent in high altitude experimental work have produced something of value to our country.

Nearly 20 years after Mac left McCook Field, he once again flew a supercharged airplane, in North Africa, when he had been recalled to active duty during World War II. As a young lieutenant checked him out for his first flight in the B-17 Flying Fortress, he explained to Mac the mechanism giving the bomber the added thrust at higher altitudes. "Know anything about this, Sir?" he asked, pointing to the supercharger control.

Mac was silent, as his mind flashed back to those hundreds of hours of test flying the turbo supercharger. He remembered the frigid cold, the lack of oxygen, and the life-threatening decrease in air pressure. "Yes," he said slowly, "I believe I do."

Epilogue

*A*FTER LEAVING THE UNITED STATES AIR SERVICE
in 1926, Mac accepted a position with Frigidaire Corporation as Assistant Chief Engineer. But the company headquarters was still in Dayton, Ohio, and as a California boy,
born and bred, Mac was anxious to return to his home
state. A few years later, when Shell Oil Company, extremely anxious
to get into the aviation business, offered Mac the new position of
organizing and heading up Shell's Aeronautical Division, he
accepted with alacrity, seeing it not only as a business opportunity,
but a chance to move back to the West. He and his young family —

wife, Nelliejay, daughters Jo-Anne, 5, and Sally, 3 — moved to San Francisco in 1929. They rented a spacious condominium high atop the hills overlooking the San Francisco Bay, at the corner of Hyde and Greenwich Streets, which also afforded them a good view of the Alameda Airport and the takeoffs and landings of Macready in his specially built $30,000 Lockheed Sirius plane, the flagship of Shell Oil's new aviation fleet.

Shell made the most of Macready's worldwide fame, keeping his name in front of the public. The interest of the nation was on aviation, and among his many published articles was a series entitled *The Future of Aviation*, which included: *Air Passenger Travel Soon to Cost Less Than Rail Travel*; *Huge Flying Boats Offer Best Possibility for Trans-Atlantic Air Travel on Regular Schedules*; *How the Airplane Will Change Our Mode of Living*; *What Kind of Jobs Aviation is Offering*; and *Aviation Has Passes From Promotion Stage to Real Business Basis*. Mac wrote articles for *National Geographic*, *Liberty*, and *Saturday Evening Post*. These articles, written in 1931, just eight years after his non-stop transcontinental flight, illustrated not only his futuristic outlook, but just how far aviation had come in such a short span of time.

Mac's office was in the Shell Oil Company building at 100 Bush Street, and according to custom, every afternoon at 4:00 work stopped and tea was served. Nelliejay and the girls tried to time their visits at that hour, to enjoy the sweet treats that accompanied the tea.

Mac's new position thrust him in the limelight of news and society, and although it was not something he was comfortable with, his inveterate shyness and modesty endeared him to the public. He recommended his long-time friend and former military pilot, Jimmy Doolittle, for the position of Eastern manager of Shell's Aviation Department, based in St. Louis, Missouri.

Mac's flights for Shell included top officers of Shell Oil Company, such as G. Leigh-Jones, President; California Governor James Rolph, Jr.; and government officials. He made public relations tours of the cities in the United States and Canada, stopping to give interviews and plug Shell aviation products. In 1931, he was appointed to the Hancock College of Aeronautics Technical Advisory Board, located at the time in Santa Maria, California.

Because of his famous name, the newspapers were anxious to give him coverage. As a consultant to cities trying to establish airport locations, Mac was much in demand for the dedication ceremonies when the airports were established. His appearance at air shows was sure to draw a crowd, for his speed records were legendary. And it was Macready who formally presented the airplane to the City of Los Angeles when the city inaugurated a flying ambulance service in June 1930. Under Mac's able direction, Shell Oil rapidly became an important factor in aviation.

One of Mac's more noteworthy flights, however, ended in disaster. He was flying the Keith Ryder plane in the Chicago Air Races in 1930. The tiny craft, weighing in at 600 pounds wringing wet, had a 20-foot wingspan, and its 130-hp engine was capable of 200 mph, according to its inventor and preliminary test flights. The wings and fuselage were plywood, with no struts, reducing wind friction in flight. Dubbed the "hummingbird," it was one of the very few planes that had been built specially for the races, and drew more attention from spectators than any other ship in the pits.

Although the little plane proved its mettle in the air race, a wing folded and the plane spiraled about drunkenly for an instant before Mac skillfully maneuvered it away from the crowd below. The plane struck with terrific force, bounced high into the air, and was demolished in the rebound. Headlines reported Macready near death from the crash, which he was. The headline "Famous Aviator Fatally Injured in Chicago Race," did not convince his wife, Nelliejay, who called every hospital in the Chicago area until she found where he was. And Mac was a long time recovering, as almost every bone in his body was broken.

Modern aero-motor commuting, as practiced by Mac, was illustrated by his first aero-motorlog trip into Yosemite. Taking off from San Francisco at 9:12 a.m., he flew to Yosemite, landing at Wawona Landing Field, where he was met by Colonel C. G. Thompson, Superintendent of Yosemite National Park, and driven to the Valley. He was back in San Francisco in time for an early dinner. And he "commuted" to see "Death Valley Scotty," to visit his "castle," which Mac described as Spanish architecture. The mansion had about 40 rooms as well as guest cottages, and was sumptuously furnished, with Oriental rugs ankle deep, gorgeous paintings, statuary, European art treasures, and endless bathrooms with exquisite tile. "There is a special room built for the organ, the ceiling alone cost $90,000 and no one in the castle can play," Mac noted. According to Mac, Scotty was thought by the locals to be a man of untold resources. In reality, however, Scotty revealed to Mac that the Death Valley ranch had been built by a wealthy insurance executive from Chicago, who Scotty had befriended through the years. "It was an astonishing revelation," to learn that the Death Valley "castle" was built with someone else's money.

Still another invitation had Mac commuting into San Simeon as a guest of William Randolph Hearst, where his dinner clothes were laid out for him (though he hadn't brought any) and where he had committed the unforgivable sin of asking his dinner partner, Kathryn Hepburn, if she was in the movies. Mac received the "cold treatment" the rest of the evening.

In Hollywood, Mac visited movie studio sets where he was introduced to the stars, including the Talmadge sisters — Constance and Norma — who thought he was "pretty cute." He was quite embarrassed when publicity pictures were taken.

Saving lives was not in Mac's job description, but on at least one occasion, in his first test flight of a new type high-speed plane, he flew a 78-year-old woman 200 miles over the Tehachipi Mountains from Los Angeles to a Tulare hospital, a flight that saved her life.

Macready was extremely active in civic affairs in San Francisco and was a member and director of the American Legion (Floyd Bennet Post), Director of the National Aeronautical Association, and member of the California State Chamber of Commerce (chairman of the Aviation Committee, Central Council), the Quiet Birdmen, Kappa Alpha Fraternity (Stanford University), the Masons, the Union League, and the Caterpillar Club. He held Transport Pilot license No. 11419.

In the spring of 1933, Mac resigned from Shell Oil Company; he wanted to move out of the city. He gave the family a vote on two choices — an extended trip around the world for a year or the purchase of a ranch. The vote was three to one for the ranch; Nelliejay was the lone holdout for the trip. Mac sent a young college man with a car and an expense account to travel all over the Western states to find the most beautiful spot for the ranch. Finally the Macready's chose a spot in the Sierras close to Yosemite National Park, where they raised race horses and cattle and ran a dude ranch for the children of their friends from San Francisco. For some years, however, Mac continued on as a consultant for Shell Oil Company.

When World War II brought Mac a recall notice from the U.S. Army Air Forces, Mac served his country once again — this time in the European Theater of Operations. When the war was over, he returned to his ranch, which by that time Nelliejay, with his power of attorney, had sold most of, an act for which he never quite forgave her. The family home was gone, and so they built another high on a hill overlooking the foothills of the Mariposa area. During those years, from 1945 to 1979, they were hosts to visitors from all over the world.

Mac died on his beloved ranch, still active and making plans for the future, in 1979.

His honors were many, including the Mackay Trophy three times, the Croix de Guerre with Palm from the French government for his World War II heroism, and enshrinement in the Aviation Hall of Fame, Dayton, Ohio, in 1968, and in the International Aerospace Hall of Fame, San Diego, California, in 1976.

Index

by Lori L. Daniel

— Aircraft —

B-17 Flying Fortress, 161
B-25, 143
Barling Bomber, 85
Capronis, 30
Curtiss
  JN-4 "Jenny" trainer, 20, 22-23
  JN4-D "Jenny" biplane, 26
DeHavilland, 78, 86, 138, 150
  DH-4, 87
  DH-4B, 106-107, 122-124, 127-131, 143-144
  DH-4B3, 131, 135, 137
  USD9AB, 32
Douglas
  C-1 Transport, 150-151
  DT-2, 149
  Observation Plane, 28, 31

Douglas *continued*
  World Cruiser, 28, 31, 145, 149
Farman, 30
Fokker, 30
  Ambulance T-2, 144
  T-2 Transport (Fokker IV), xiii, 1-2, 16-17, 28-29, 46-52, 54, 57-64, 66-69, 74-77, 95, 97-98, 100, 111-114, 117-118, 120, 144-145, 148, 151
Gerhardt Cycle Plane, 33
Hummingbird, 164
Le Pére LUSAC-11, 36-40, 42-43, 89-91
Lockheed Sirius, 163
Loening Amphibian COA AS 24-8, 105, 148
MB-3 biplane, 31, 36, 69-71, 78, 95-96
Nieuport, 30
Sopwith Camel, 30

Spad, 30
Sperry Verville Racer, 95
Stout Air Pullman, 148
VCP-R (Racer) Verville-Packard biplane, 20
Wright Flyer, 107-108
XCO-5 biplane, 104, 152-156

— A —

Ackerman, Lieutenant, 47
Aero Club of America, 63
Ainsworth, C. E., 137
Air Mail, 133, 157
Air Service Engineering School, 146
Alaska, 149, 152
    Chignik, 149
    Cordova, 149
    Ketchikan, 149
    Point Barrow, 151
    Sitka, 149
Alibi Trophy, 47
altitude
    American, 155
    world record, 45, 65, 94, 107, 155
America, 18, 30, 107, 112, 131, 149
    East Coast, 52
    Midwest, 48, 55
    Northwest, 31
    Pacific Coast, 66, 68, 112, 155
    West, 17, 61, 162
American, xiv, 20, 55, 113, 148
American Legion (Floyd Bennet Post), 165
Amis, Lieutenant, 32, 84
Annals of Flight, 112
Arctic, 150-151, 154
Argentine, 149
Arizona, 11, 14, 58, 112
    Bowie, 58
    Chloride, 14
    Dragoon Mountains, 58
    Holbrook, 130
    Kingman, 14
    Meteor Crater, 140
    Old Trails Road, 14
    Painted Desert, 140
    Petrified Forest, 140
    Phoenix, 76-77, 112
    Show Low, 112
    St. Johns, 76-77
    Tucson, 57-58, 60
    Wickenburg, 112
Armistice, 27
around-the-world-flight, 149

Arvada Ferry, 14
Associated Press, 59
Atlantic Ocean, 107
aviator glasses, xiv

— B —

Bacon, John L. (Mayor), 51
Bane, Thurman H. (Colonel), 34, 36, 48, 89
Barksdale, Hoy (Lieutenant), 32, 84, 118, 158
barograph chart, 93
Barry, R. Smith (Colonel), 26
Beck, Ma, 18
Berger, Adolph, 89, 104
Blake, Dean, 56
boom town, 7
Bossoutrot, Lieutenant, 55
British, 149
    Royal Air Force, 26
Brookley, Wendell (Lieutenant), 47, 118
Bruner, Donald L., 132-133
Burdick, Kirk, 8, 10
Bureau of Standards, 44, 157
Burma, 149
Bye, George T. 150

— C —

Cabell, R. H., 11
California, 112, 127, 139, 162-163
    Berkeley, 19-20
        University of California, 19
            School of Military Aeronautics, 19
    California Valley, 112
    Catalina Island, 117
    Death Valley, 128, 139, 164-165
    Goffs, 8, 19
    Hollywood, 128, 165
    Laguna Mountains, 52
    Lake Tahoe, 139
    Los Angeles, 3-4, 6-9, 15, 19, 71, 74, 80,
        115, 127-128, 157, 164-165
        Berenda School, 3
        Pico Heights, 3
    Mariposa, 166
    Mount Shasta, 139
    Mount Tamalpais, 139
    Mount Whitney, 128, 139
    Mount Wilson, 128
    Palo Alto, 81
        Stanford University, 4, 8-9, 70, 81
            Kappa Alpha Fraternity, 81, 165
                Alumnae Association, 81

California *continued*
  Redding, 127
  Sacramento, 127
  Salmon Alps, 139
  San Bernardino, 5
  San Diego, xi, xiii, 3, 20, 25, 46, 48-55, 57,
    59, 62, 64, 69, 74-75, 100-101, 112-113,
    117-118, 127, 146, 166
    Ballast Point Lighthouse, 51
    Chamber of Commerce, 21
    Hotel del Coronado, 117
    International Aerospace Hall of Fame,
      166
    North Island, xiii, 52, 54, 111, 113
      North Island Naval Air Base, 50
      Rockwell Field, 18, 20, 25, 50-52, 54,
        57, 113, 117, 127
    Point Loma, 57
    University Club, 56
    U. S. Grant Hotel, 50, 117
  San Diego Bay, 51
  San Francisco, 19, 133, 145-147, 163-165
    Alameda Airport, 163
  San Francisco Bay, 19, 163
  San Simeon, 165
  Santa Maria, 163
    Hancock College of Aeronautics
      Technical Advistory Board, 113
  Santa Monica, 128
  Sequoia National Park, 139
  Sierra Nevada Mountains, 49, 165
  Skiddoo, 128
  Southern California, 11, 127-128
  State Chamber of Commerce, 165
  Tehachipi Mountains, 165
  Temecula Pass, 52, 57
  Tulare, 165
  Yosemite National Park, 127, 139, 164-165
    Wawona Landing Field, 164
Call Bulletin (San Francisco), 25
Callizo, M., 154
Canada, 2, 9, 139, 163
  British Columbia
    Prince Rupert, 149
Carver, H. B., 35
Cashman, Jim, 13-14
Catalpa Sphinx Moth, 35-36, 86
Caterpillar Club, 79, 137, 165
Chicago Air Races, 15, 164
China
  Hong Kong, 145, 149
Civil War, 30

Clark
  Judge, 119
  Mrs., 119
Clark County Republican Central Committee,
  14
Collier's Magazine, 25
Colorado River Reclamation Project, 129
Connell, Tom, 10-12
copper, 4
Croix de Guerre with Palm, 166
crop dusting, xi, xiv, 34-36, 86, 159
Crumrine, Clarence (Lieutenant), 46-47

— D —
Dade, Colonel, 20-21
Davis, Secretary, 151
Dayton Aircraft Corporation, 158
Dayton Evening Herald, 94
Dempsey, Jack, 31
Denmark, 27
DePalma, Ralph, 29-30
Detroit Aviation Society, 149, 151
Dichman, Ernest W., 49
distance record, world, 61, 65, 107
Doolittle, James H. "Jimmy" (Lieutenant),
  xiv, 84, 105, 142-151, 163
Dormoy, Etienne, 34-36
Douglas, Donald, 28, 31
Droupin, Lieutenant, 55
Dumbbell Trophy, 84
Dunn, Fred, 6-7
Dutch, 48, 119

— E —
Endurance flight
  record, xi, 53-55, 62, 64, 107
  world record, xi, 52, 65
Engine
  Curtiss OX-5, 20
  Liberty, 1-2, 17, 37-40, 49, 54, 59, 62-63,
    113, 148-150, 156, 158
England
  Gosport, 26
    Royal Air Force School of Flying, 26
  London, 149
English, 7
Ervin, Captain, 52-53
Europe, 13, 18
European, 149
European Theater of Operations, 165
Evans, Mr., 150

— F —

Fairchild, 158
Fairchild, Muir, 78
Fédération Aéronautique Internationale
  (FAI), 40, 44, 55, 63, 155-156
Fisher, Mr., 4-7
flying ambulance service, 164
Fokker, Anthony, 119-120
Ford Motor Company, 150, 157-158, 160
France, 154
  LaBourget, 55
  Paris, 40, 149
Frank, Major, 149
French, 38, 40, 52, 55, 62, 149, 166
  Aerial Federation, 55
  Aero Club, 55
Frigidaire Corporation, 162

— G —

General Electric, 155-156
General Motors Corporation, 159
George Palmer Putnam, Inc., 150
Gerhardt, Fred, 33
German, 49, 143
Gilmore, Brigadier General, 107
gold, 4-7, 139
Goodyear, 49
Gosport System, 26
Gossard, H. A., 34-36
Grand Canyon, 124, 129, 139
  Observatory Peak, 124
Great Divide, 58
Great Lakes, 152
Greenland, 149
Guam, 145-146

— H —

Harding, Warren G. (President), 113, 119
Harris
  Harold, 78-79, 157
  Lieutenant, 47, 137
Hawaii, 146
  Honolulu, 145-147
Hearst, William Randolph, 165
Henderson, Paul (Colonel), 157
Hennick, Carl "Slim," 16-17
Hepburn, Kathryn, 165
Himalayas, 151
Hopkins, C. W. (Colonel), 6-7
Hubbard, Mr., 4-7
Hudson Bay, 2
Hudson Bay High, 2, 61

Huff-Daland Dusters, Inc., 157
Hutchinson, Lieutenant, 32, 84

— I —

Iceland
  Reykjavik, 149
Idaho
  Blackfoot Range, 124
  Boise, 125
  Caribou Range, 124
  Pocatello, 123
  Sawtooth Mountains, 139
Illinois, 60
  Belleville, 67
    Scott Field, 67
  Chicago, 133, 158, 164
  Monmouth, 158
  Springfield, 132
India
  Calcutta, 149
Indian, 69, 139
Indiana, 66
  Fort Benjamin Harrison, 60-61
    Schoen Field, 60
  Indianapolis, 47, 57, 60-61, 66
    Indianapolis Speedway, 60
  Richmond, 47
  Terre Haute, 66, 148
Iowa
  Iowa City, 123
Iraq
  Bagdad, 149
Italian, 149
Italy, 21

— J —

Japan, 149
  Tokyo, 143
Johnson, Lieutenant, 32, 84
Jones
  Bradley (Lieutenant), 147
  Captain, 29-30
Joukowsky StAe-27-A wings, 153

— K —

Kansas, 48, 59-60, 68
  Wichita, 57, 68
Kelly, G. Oakley, xiii, 1-2, 16-18, 28, 46-64,
  67-68, 76, 97-99, 101, 112-114, 116-117,
  159
Kelly Tires, 53
Kenney, Franklin R. (Colonel), 17, 114

Klegal, Pete, 129
Knights of the Air, 155

— L —

Langham, Roy, 41-42
Langley and Wright Brothers Airways, 51
Leigh-Jones, G., 163
Lewis, Meriwether, 139
Liberty, 163
Lindbergh, Charles A. (Colonel), xiv, 107, 121
Lockwood, R. G. (Lieutenant), 32, 84
Loening, Grover, 105, 148
Louisiana
    Lake Charles, 23
        Gerstner Field, 18, 23-25
            School for Instructors, 23

— M —

Mackay Trophy, xi, xiv, 65, 109-110, 160, 166
Macready
    Benjamin "Ben," 3-9, 11, 13-14, 50, 72, 74, 80, 82
        Justice of the Peace, 7
    George, 9
    Jo-Anne, 120, 163
    John A. "Mac" (Lieutenant), xi, xiii-xiv, 1-4, 7-10, 15-18, 20-30, 46-47, 80-82, 84-88, 90-91, 93-94, 97-99, 101-103, 105-109, 111-122, 134-138, 162-166
        amateur boxer, 4, 70, 155
        aviation achievements, xi
        experimental pilot, 69-78
        Justice of the Peace, 9-14, 82
        photo expedition, 123-133, 139-141
        test pilot, 31-45, 48-64, 66-68, 89, 96, 104, 142, 144-161
    Mattie Delahunt Beck, 3, 9, 12, 50, 55, 72-73, 80, 116
    Nelliejay, 102-103, 118-120, 131, 137, 163-165
        see also Turner, Nelliejay
    Sally, 163
Maitland, Lester (Lieutenant), 118, 155
Maltman, Johnny, 3-4
Mammoth Hot Springs, 125
Manila, 145-146
Manual of Administration of an Air Service Flying School, 26
Marshall, Fred, 144
Martin, Jue, 9-10
Masons, 165

Massachusetts
    Boston, 6, 144, 149
Massachusetts Institute of Technology (M.I.T.), 143, 145
Mather, Stephen, 137-138
McCarroll, H. G., 150-151
McDougal, Harry, 123-124
McIntosh, Major, 144-145, 147-148
McIntyre, Doc, 13
McMahon, T. C. (Lieutenant), 46-47
Meeker, Ezra, 113
Meister, Louis "Louie," 32-33, 84
Mexico
    Ensenada, 122, 127
Michigan
    Detroit, 150-151
Midway Island, 145-146
Miller, Max, 22-23
Mine
    Bishop, 7
    New Era, 4
    Quaker Girl Group, 7
    Santa Fe, 7
    Saturn, 7
    St. Louis, 7
    The Quartette District, 7-8, 82, 129
Missouri, 60
    Jefferson City, 67
    Kansas City, 67-68, 117
    Ozark Mountains, 2
    St. Louis, 50, 57, 60, 117, 148, 163
Mitchell, William E. "Billy" (Brigadier General), 36-37, 41, 143, 152
Moffett, Lieutenant, 32, 84
Molly, 69-71, 73
Montana, 138, 140
    Big Timber, 140
    Glacier National Park, 139
    Kalispell, 139
    Lake McDonald, 139
    Lewis' Glacier Park Hotel, 139
Moriarity, Pat, 73-74
Morin, H. E., 51
Moseley, Corliss C., 20, 157
Moss, Sanford (Dr.), 89
Mount Adams, 125-126
Mount Everest, 150-152
Mount McKinley, 152

— N —

National Aeronautical Association, 53, 110, 165

National Cash Register Company, 160
National Geographic, 94, 163
Nebraska
    North Platte, 123
    Omaha, 123
Neidermeyer, F. W. "Neidy" (Lieutenant), 77-78
Neille, C. R., 34
Netherlands, 49
Nevada, 6-7, 11, 13-14, 18
    Arrowhead Trail, 14
    Boulder Canyon, 140
    Carson City, 139
    Comstock Lode, 139
    El Dorado Canyon, 13
    Grand Canyon, Northern Rim, 140
    Great Salt Lake, 139
    Kings River Canyon, 140
    Las Vegas, 13, 128-129
    Mount Charleston, 140
    Reno, 18, 19, 80, 139
        Riverside Hotel, 19
    Searchlight, 3-4, 7-10, 12-15, 18, 82, 129
        Kennedy House Hotel, 18
        Main Street, 4, 8, 10-11
        Searchlight Bench and Bar, 11
        Wellington Saloon, 8-9, 13
        Yellowstone Saloon, 18
    Virginia City, 139
    Wasatch Mountains, 139
New Mexico, 48, 68-69
    Carrizozo, 58
    Deming, 58
    Malpals lava beds, 58
    San Andres Mountains, 58
    Santa Rosa, 54, 76, 112
    Tecolote, 58
    Tucumcari, 53, 57, 59, 69
New York, 31-32, 46, 51, 56, 111, 113, 123, 133, 154
    Coney Island, 17
    Ithaca, 69-70, 96
        Cornell University, 70, 96
    Long Island, xiii, 1, 25, 48, 57, 114
        Hazelhurst Field, 16-17
        Mineola Field, 25
        Mitchell Field, 20, 57
        Roosevelt Field, xiii, 1, 16-17
        Roosevelt Raceway, 16
        Westbury, 16
    New York City, 113, 152
New York Tribune, 51

New York Union, 51
New York World, 51
night flying, 132-133
    ground lights, 133
    landing light, 132
North Africa, 161
North Pole, 117, 149
Norway
    Spitzbergen, 151

— O —

OAT (outside air temperature), 91
Ocher, Major, 23-24
Ohio, 47, 55, 131
    Casstown, 35
    Cleveland, 158
        Parks Department, 34
    Columbus, 72, 131-133
        Miramar Restaurant, 72
        Norton Field, 133
    Dayton, xi, 2, 20, 29-31, 41, 47, 57, 62-64, 66, 69, 78, 83-84, 105, 107-108, 117-118, 120, 122, 128, 131-134, 136-137, 142-143, 150, 156-159, 162, 166
        Aviation Hall of Fame, 166
        Canoe Club, 144
        Chamber of Commerce, 136
        Dayton Community Country Club, 134
        Dayton View, 143
        Hills and Dales section, 120, 134
        Lebanon Pike Highway, 137
        McCook Field, xiv, 28-31, 33-34, 36, 38-40, 44, 46-48, 53, 61, 63, 73, 77-78, 83-84, 89, 117, 131-134, 137, 139, 142-145, 147-148, 150-155, 157, 159-161
        McCook Field Hospital, 38
        McCook Museum, 44, 105
        North Riverdale Street, 143
        Sutmillers Nightclub and Restaurant, 144
        Wilbur Wright Field, 63, 85, 158-159
    New Carlyle, 63
    Ohio State University, 72
        Kappa Alpha Theta, 72
    Toledo, 31-32
    Troy, xi, 35, 86
Ohio Department of Entomology, 34-35
Oklahoma, 48, 57, 59
    Lawton, 50, 117
O'Mara, _____, 51
Oregon
    Mount Hood, 127, 139

Ormabee, _____, 51
Ostfriesland (German ship), 143

— P —

Packard, 37
Pacific Ocean, 147
Pakistan
    Karachi, 149
Panama, 159
parachute, 42, 70, 77-79, 131, 135-138
    flares, 131, 133
    jump, 79, 159
        night, xi, xiv, 135-136
Parker, Clark, 14
Parmafee, E. F., 51
Patrick, Mason M. (Major General), 48, 61,
    64, 113, 122, 137, 144-145, 147-151, 159-
    160
Pennsylvania, 17-18, 47
    McKeesport, 158
    Pittsburgh, 57
Pennzoil motor oil, 50
Philippines, 146
photography, aerial, xi, 107, 138-139, 151
    expedition of America, xi, xiv, 123-128,
        130-132, 137-139, 153, 159
    solar eclipse, xi, xiv, 122
Pickering, Loring, 25
Porter, Otis, 63
Portuguese, 149
Powell, Hartford, 25
Pratt
    Conger (Colonel), 25
    E. L., 33
pressurized cockpit, xiv, 44, 92
Price, John, 143-144
Prince Axel, 27
Private Pilot Manual, 26
Pulitzer Trophy, 20

— Q —

Quiet Birdmen, 165

— R —

Richardson, D. G., 24
Rickenbacker, 158
River
    Arkansas, 68
    Canadian, 59
    Colorado, 14, 57, 112
    Columbia, 125, 127, 139
    Miami, 30, 83, 159

River *continued*
    Missouri, 68
    Rio Grande, 58, 76
    Salt, 112
    Yellowstone, 124, 139
        Upper Fall, 124
Rock Springs Land and Cattle Company, 14
Rolph, Jr., James, 163
Russell, Jack, 7
Ryder, Keith, 15, 164

— S —

Sam (miner), 4
San Diego Union, 51
Santa Fe Mining Company, 13
Saturday Evening Post, 163
Schroeder, Rudolph "Shorty," 38, 157
Scotland, 149
Scottish, 3, 6, 8, 69
Scotty, Death Valley, 164
Seligson, Lamar, 25
Shell Oil Company, 50, 162-165
    Aeronautical Division, 162-163
Siam, 149
Skoning, Duke, 25
Smith
    Commander, 143
    Dean, 22, 24-25
solar eclipse
    see photography, aerial
Soup Flight, 61
South America, 149
Southern Nevada Mill, 13
Southern Pacific Railroad, 57
space flight, 159
Spanish, 164
Sperry-Messenger, 31
Standard Oil, 25
Stefansson, Vilhjalmur, 150, 154
Stevens, A. W. (Captain), 106-107, 122-131,
    137-141, 151
Stiff, Joe, 77, 135, 137
Stout, William B., 148-149
Studebaker Securities Company, 158
Swickard, Jim, 4-6
Swope, William Bayard, 51

— T —

Talmadge
    Constance, 165
    Norma, 165
transcontinental flight, 147

transcontinental flight *continued*
  non-stop, xi, xiii-xiv, 1, 48, 61, 64, 95, 99-
    101, 113-114, 117, 122, 153, 159, 163
  night air route, 133, 159
transPacific flight, 105, 142-145, 148-149
test pilot, 29-32, 34, 36-38, 48, 78, 84, 88,
  115, 118, 133, 142-143, 152, 155, 157, 160
Texas, 59
  Corpus Christi, 25
  El Paso, 49-50, 117-118
  San Antonio, 25
    Brooks Field, 18, 25, 27
*The All Thru System of Flying Instruction as
  Taught at Brooks Field*, 26
The Flying McCooks, 30
The Future of Aviation, 163
The New York Times, 153
Thomas Morse Chain Works, 31, 36
Thomas Morse Company, 69-70, 95-96
Thompson
  C. G. (Colonel), 164
  Charles (Reverend), 116
Tourtellot, Lieutenant, 32, 84
Tripett, Oscar, 32
Turner
  Laura, 71
  Nelliejay, 71-75, 113, 115-117
    see also Macready, Nellijay

— U —

Union League, 165
United States, xiv, 18, 42, 45, 48, 63, 80, 95,
  100-101, 138, 154, 163
  Army, 30, 37, 49, 138, 143-144, 159
    Air Corps, 44
    Air Forces, 165
    Air Service, xiv, 1-2, 17, 19, 25-26, 34,
      36, 40, 47-49, 55, 80, 84, 88, 114, 117,
      120, 122-123, 132-133, 137-138, 143,
      147-149, 151, 159-160, 162
    Regular, 22
  Cavalry, 18-20
  Department of Agriculture, 34, 86
  National Guard, 32
  Navy, 113, 128, 143-144, 149
  Post Office Department, 157-158
  Public Park Service, 138
  Signal Corps, 19-20
Utah
  Bryce Canyon, 139-140
  Cedar Breaks, 140

Utah *continued*
  Zion National Park, 140

— V —

Van Duzer School of Boxing, 3
Vince (miner), 8
Virginia, 11

— W —

Wake Island, 145-146
Walton, Leo, 25
Washington, 125, 151
  Mount Rainier, 125-127
  Olympic Mountains, 139
  Seattle, 149
  Vancouver, 125-127
Washington, D.C., 19, 56, 61, 109, 117, 137,
  144, 148-149
  Air and Space Museum, 110
  Mayflower Hotel, 150
  Smithsonian Institution, 112, 145
Waterman, Waldo, 20
Watson, Mary, 50-51, 54-56
Weather Bureau, 2, 56
Weeks, John W., 117
West Coast Golden Gloves Championship, 4
Western Air Express, 157
West Point, 25
Weyant, R. G., 158
Wheatley, John, 12
Whitten, Senator, 125
Wildman, Doc, 21
Wilkins, Hubert (Sir), 149-150
Willard, Jess, 31
Willard-Dempsey fight, 31
World War I, 14, 18, 30, 49, 123, 132, 143,
  149
World War II, 21, 143, 161, 165-166
Wright Brothers, 30, 69, 149
  Orville, xi, xiv, 40-42, 44, 63-64, 107-108,
    155-157
Wuichet, Ed, 136-137
Wyoming, 124
  Cheyenne, 123, 133
  Jackson Hole, 139
  Rock Springs, 123
  Yellowstone National Park, 123-125, 139

— Y —

Yukutat Bay, 149